AT THE EDGE OF TOMORROW

As AI and automation advance, are humans becoming redundant in the modern workplace?

Unleashing Human Potential in the AI Era

Deepa Venkateswaran Mukherjee, PhD

INDIA · SINGAPORE · MALAYSIA

ISBN 979-8-89186-438-2

"At the Edge of Tomorrow" brilliantly captures the essence of today's rapid technological advancement, illustrating how empowering employees through reskilling leads to exceptional customer experiences. Deepa's groundbreaking model for nurturing a culture of continuous learning are pivotal for businesses aiming to uplift traditional employee engagement and drive customer experience to new heights. This essential guide is a timely beacon for organizations striving to excel in the new tech-centric workplace by fostering collaboration and embracing change."

– Ron Kaufman

Global Keynote Speaker | NYT Bestselling Author of "Uplifting Service" | Ranked World's #1 Customer Experience Guru

"An empowering call to action to preserve the essence of human talent in the modern workplace, where each one can shape the future of work, regardless of technological change; for all positive evolution has at its core the wisdom of the human heart."

– Dr. Harbeen Arora Rai

Founder & President, G100 Club, ALL Ladies League (ALL), Women Economic Forum (WEF), WICCI - Women's Indian Chamber of Commerce and Industry, SHEconomy

"The industrial age led to the design of educational structures that cultivated the compliant learner, a model that is no longer relevant, effective, nor efficient in meeting individual, organizational, or societal needs. The global trends and new workplace contexts, demand a self-directed and lifelong learning populace that can maximize technological tools and capitalize on the amazing capacity of humans. Deepa Mukherjee's description of reskilling research and the intriguing model for leveraging employee self-skilling abilities in workplaces can help self-directed learning enthusiasts explore a new dimension during the ongoing industrial transformation."

– Dr. Naomi Boyer

Chair, International Society for
Self-Directed Learning

"We are at an interesting intersection of Humans and Machines and like all intersections and transitioning phases this could be confusing for many and exciting for some. 'At the Edge of Tomorrow' explores the agency we have to self-skill us in this transitioning phase. Deepa's academic vigour combined with her years of experience in tech organisations make this book a compelling read."

– Santhosh Babu

Founder of OD Alternatives and Orglens | Management Thinker,
Culture Expert

"Deepa has been one of the foremost authorities in the corporate learning space with her 2+ decades of in-depth industry experience. Building a sustainable learning culture for large tech organisations over time has enabled her with unique insights on the space of unlearning, relearning, and self- learning. This book is a must read for all industry leaders who are looking to build a learning organisation, one where employees show a higher degree of self-initiative, align their development journey to a fast-changing disruptive world, and avoid the landmines of obsolescence and irrelevance that are strewn along the way."

– John Cherian

MD & CEO Enparadigm, Transforming Talent for the
Future of Work

In the heart of the digital age, where AI and automation redraw the boundaries of work, At the Edge of Tomorrow stands as a critical guide for navigating the seismic shifts of Industry 4.0 and beyond.

This book is a clarion call to the workforce of today and tomorrow. With precise and scholarly insights, it unveils the stark reality: a world where the relentless march of technology risks rendering human skills redundant and obsolete. Yet, within the pages lies a powerful counter-narrative, one of hope, resilience, and adaptability.

Discover transformative models and groundbreaking strategies for individuals and businesses amidst this chaos of change, vital for sustaining human relevance in the AI-dominated landscape.

At the Edge of Tomorrow is not just about understanding the future, it is about seizing it. It is a manifesto for lifelong learners, business innovators, and visionary leaders. The future is unforgiving, the question is, are you prepared?

Dive in, and emerge ready to claim your place in the dawn of Industry 5.0

Dedication

This book is dedicated to the almighty who has blessed human beings with infinite potential to learn continuously and evolve from adversities.

Contents

PART I
Great Skills Disruption and the Reskilling Revolution

PART II
Understanding Reskilling & Related Subject Areas

PART III
Employee Self Skilling, Reskilling, & Future of Work

▶ Contents ◀

Acknowledgements

The research content of this book has been taken from my doctoral thesis. I thank the authorities at Amity University, the faculty of management studies, and most importantly my research supervisors for their guidance and support during my PhD study. I thank all my industry colleagues, PhD guides, and co-guides who wholeheartedly supported me by sharing their experiences and insights at different stages of my research journey. Their intellect and wisdom reflects in this work. I also thank the editorial team of Notion Press for their support during this process. Above all, I would like to convey my never-ending gratitude towards my family, my parents for the selfless love and care that they have always blessed me with, my dear husband for being my pillar of strength at all times, and to the two angel energizers of my life – my adorable children Aditya and Aarav for keeping me upbeat in my life with their pure and immense love.

Who Should Read This Book

Reskilling people for the new jobs of modern workplaces is a top priority for every business and nation. The limitations-in both pace and scale- associated with traditional methods are acknowledged by stakeholders. Both industry and academic communities' interest in this highly under-researched subject is on the rise owing to its relevance to the modern world of work. The contents of this book are a useful resource for management researchers working in areas related to skilling and employment. It is an essential read that can help business leaders and HR professionals as they work on new talent strategies to leverage human capital for achieving competitive advantage during the ongoing industrial transformations. I personally would recommend every college student looking to enter the world of work, as well as, every working professional who is already a part of the workforce to read this book and acquaint themselves with one of the most significant crises being faced by the industrial world that is likely to have a prolonged and lasting impact on mankind.

Industry 5.0 envisages a new socio-economic era with sustainable, human centric, and resilient business models. It seeks to add human aspects and include sustainability goals while adopting robots, smart machines, AI, IOT, and big data to work alongside people. These technologies have disrupted the industrial world and paved way to what we are dealing with currently – the Industrial Revolution 4.0. The IR 4.0 has brought with it the 'reskilling revolution' in the world of work. Jobs are getting redefined at scale due to the phenomenal change in humans' and machines' share as well as quality of tasks with the rapid adoption of these technologies. It is estimated that almost fifty percent of the working population is expected to get de-skilled and run out of paid work and employment in the near future. Being unemployed has greater consequences on individuals and society than simply a loss of earning capacity. However, it is acknowledged that displaced workers can be saved from adverse consequences if they can be prepared for the jobs of tomorrow by effective reskilling. Organizations can proactively enable the transitioning of workers into sustainable job opportunities. Maintaining the employability of the working population is of utmost importance towards the well-being of any population. This also promotes the growth of businesses with the supply of talent against new emerging jobs. The increasing rate of technological advancement is decreasing the shelf life of skills for jobs. These developments hint towards a future where workforce reskilling will be an ongoing need for every business and a lifelong phenomenon for the future of work. Reskilling for IR 4.0 will move humans away from mechanical jobs to more meaningful and creative jobs and will also create way for Industry 5.0. Human resource management for Industry 5.0 includes culture building for continuous workforce upskilling and reskilling as a prerequisite for future proofing economic and societal development. Individuals play an agentic role in these reskilling journeys. Elucidating on the subject of reskilling, the role of individuals, organizations, and governments across nations, and understanding the factors and determinants that make reskilling efforts successful, has therefore become essential for business owners and HR professionals as they build their talent strategies.

What started a few years ago as a quest to find a solution for reskilling IT workers with redundant primary skills turned into a life-changing journey for me. Like most of my other peer leaders in the Learning & Development fraternity, I brought in new ideas in my organization to deal with the global talent crisis when the skills canvass changed entirely. I realized that the skills businesses were looking for to assist their growth were changing significantly. One of the biggest challenges the industry was struggling with was this typical chicken-or-egg dilemma – whether to train people or get the business first. Being the L&D leader of my firm, I assumed the responsibility of striking the balance between enabling the business and parallelly protecting relevance for people whose skills were becoming outdated. Not that I didn't taste initial success, but there were more impending issues I struggled with – the biggest of which was the heterogeneous nature of the problem and the mismatch in pace with business. As I went deeper into the subject, the broader areas opened for me to discover the ocean of new possibilities to be explored. Like Rhonda Byrne says in 'The Secret', it seemed now that the universe transpired, and I had discovered my life's purpose. This was probably the turning point where I directed my energies towards a bigger cause.

In the months that followed, I found myself exploring, gathering info, collaborating with other experts, and experimenting. Many friends and colleagues in the industry volunteered to support me with their wisdom and experience as I started my systematic doctoral research on the subject. Through this book I bring to you the insights I could draw from my research thesis. I have divided the contents into three parts. Part I introduces the ongoing reskilling revolution in the industry, and the situation in India. Part II highlights what we know about the process of reskilling, the various theories, concepts, and models in related areas that can help us to understand the phenomenon with a scientific approach. It calls out the agentic role of individuals and the importance of individual self-skilling in the process of reskilling and presents the Employee Self-Skilling Model (ESSM)®. ESSM® can be used by organizations to leverage individual employees' self-skilling as a tool for employee reskilling within their organization. ESSM® is empirically validated and presents factors of employee self-skilling that determine over 70% of the outcomes of employee reskilling. Focusing on these factors while building talent strategies will hence enable organizations to leverage employee's role effectively in their reskilling initiatives. Finally, Part III of the book discusses Human Resource Management for Industry 5.0 with a new dimension of employee reskilling and adoption of circular talent management for sustainable development. If you are a business owner or HR leader, I hope the contents of this book are useful to you as you build your talent strategies to be ready for the future of work. If you are a management researcher, I hope you can use the content to advance research further on the subject. The book equips the reader with a comprehensive collation of available literature on the subject, besides presenting alternatives and opportunities that may be explored to help humans remain relevant in the age of AI and automation. By using the Employee Self Skilling Model presented in this book, organizations can build a self-sustaining model for reskilling and lifelong learning of employees. This book lays the foundation for individual career self-governance in the 21st century world of work. While it might seem more relevant to business/HR leaders of organizations and management students, researchers, and consultants at the face of it, any working professional or student can benefit by reading it to understand the new world of work that they are entering, the importance and knowledge about skilling to remain employable. Through this book, I make a modest attempt to share my learnings from almost three decades of being in the space of people skilling, career development, and employment. It is a humble call for collective and collaborative action towards a glaring problem that, if not appropriately addressed, is likely to impact everyone on the planet at some point or the other.

"Environmental and economic sustainability are areas that have been worked on extensively. This initiative strives to serve the increasingly essential purpose of individual professional sustainability. What we get to do together will be stepping stones for reaching new heights of efficient and positive human resource management in the decades to come."

Introduction

"Ensure inclusive education and promote lifelong learning opportunities for all"

"Promote inclusive & sustainable economic growth, employment and decent work"

– Extracted from United Nations Sustainable Development Goals 4 and 8

Sustainable development is development which meets the needs of humankind for the present without compromising the ability of the future generations to meet their own resource needs. While the principles of sustainable development are rooted in earlier ideas of preservation of natural resources that emerged to address environmental concerns in the twentieth century, the discipline has evolved and now focuses on the three realms of economic development, social development, and environmental protection for future generations. With this evolution it brings to the fore social sustainability that relates with people. The most fundamental resource of any organization or nation is its people – in other words, the "Human Resource". All other resources become significant only when people extract their usefulness. It is people, with their needs, demands, skills, and abilities, who turn other resources useful for the organization, society, and economy. Development and economic performance of nations is driven by the successful management of their resource wealth. The United Nations (UN), the world's largest intergovernmental organization that aims at harmonizing the actions of nations across the globe towards the larger good for humanity, established a blueprint to achieve a better and more sustainable future for all people and the world in the year 2015 in the form of Sustainability Development Goals. Sustainable Development Goals (SDGs) are seventeen interlinked global goals laid out by the United Nations. They are.

   i.   No Poverty,
   ii. Zero Hunger,
   iii. Good Health and Well-being,
   iv. Quality Education,
   v.   Gender Equality
   vi. Clean Water and Sanitation,
   vii. Affordable and Clean Energy,
   viii. Decent Work and Economic Growth,
   ix. Industry, Innovation, and Infrastructure,
   x.   Reduced Inequality,
   xi. Sustainable cities and communities,
   xii. Responsible Consumption and Production,
   xiii. Climate Action,
   xiv. Life Below Water,
   xv. Life on Land,
   xvi. Peace, Justice, and Strong Institutions,
   xvii. Partnership for the Goals.

Goals 4 and 8 are concerned with ensuring inclusive opportunities for education, decent work, and employment for all of mankind irrespective of anyone's social or economic status, life stage, age, gender, ethnicity, or any differentiating aspect for that matter. Work and employment structure our lives and are not purely a means to an economic end. Beyond monetary income, intrinsic rewards like sense of worth, and the want of 'what I can do' are more important for human beings. The perceived value and meaning of work, however, keeps changing. Leisure ethics replace work ethic and fuel technological advancement and automation to simplify work. Alienation of work, minimizing autonomy and easy transitions to automated alternatives for improving profitability and efficiency are characteristic of businesses and growth. The advent of capitalism and technology have been cited as causes for the industrial revolutions. The three industrial revolutions, besides bringing an increase in global income and improved quality of life for people across the world, also brought with them deskilling, reskilling, and new employment. However, the current industrial revolution has additionally brought with it the 'reskilling revolution'. Almost 50% of the working population is expected to get deskilled and run out of paid work and employment in a short span of time. Besides the loss of capacity to earn a living, unemployment has further negative consequences. According to the Society for the Psychological Study of Social Issues, individuals who are unemployed have lesser family and marital satisfaction and increased family challenges compared to employed people. Rise in unemployment has been correlated with increase in societal concerns like crime rates, suicides, broken marriages, drug addiction, and depression.

The combined health and economic shocks of 2020 owing to the COVID-19 pandemic fully exposed the inadequacies of our social contracts. Economies across the globe witnessed a freefall and mass disruption in labour markets. Millions of people globally lost their livelihoods and millions more are at risk from global recession, structural change to the economy and further automation. Income inequalities and technology-driven displacement of jobs has been a growing concern since the emergence of the industrial era. However, the unprecedented scale of the current crisis demands a global reset of the socio-economic system. The World Economic Forum in its Future of Jobs Report 2020 suggests that these technological innovations that define the changes in the current era, can also be leveraged to unleash human potential. We can protect displaced workers from dire situations and orient them towards the jobs of tomorrow by reskilling. There is an urgent need to proactively enable the transitioning of workers into sustainable job opportunities. It is also evident that building a culture for continuous workforce upskilling and reskilling is a prerequisite for future proofing economic and societal development. It is the time when businesses, governments, and workers need to work together to implement a new vision for the global workforce. The future of work is already here. Embracing uncertainty, lifelong learning, and acquiring new skills is a necessity in every worker's life. With the shrinking of available time to attain proficiency in new skills, it is essential to look for new methods of reskilling individuals that can deliver desired learning outcomes at scale. Interestingly the same disruptive technologies also offer solutions to meet this unprecedent massive reskilling goals of the economic world. Besides the quantum and scale of the reskilling needs, these technologies offer disruptive speed with their outreach – which is important as the time available for reskilling is also shrinking amidst the challenges pertaining to the COVID-19 pandemic and rapid technology adoption.

Protecting people in this context is a necessity for sustainable development. It matters equally to businesses in the short term as it does in the long term. This is because employees in organizations are more loyal to and productive for the business when they feel respected, cared for, and safe for themselves. 'Sustainable Development' is a phrase now widely used in many government documents and has three parts: environment, social, and economic sustainability as shown by the Venn diagram in Figure 1.1: Scheme of Sustainable Development. The diagram depicts that Sustainable Development ties together the concern for carrying capacity of natural systems with the social and economic challenges faced by humanity. The

SDGs are a universal call to action to meet human development goals without undermining the planetary integrity and the stability of natural systems. While much of the work done and progress achieved so far towards sustainable development have focused on the environmental and more basic social goals, the mushrooming danger of mid-career unemployment, early retirement, and frequent upskilling and reskilling needed at a massive scale globally across industries is grossly under addressed.

This book is an attempt to attract the attention of business owners, HR professionals, researchers, and stakeholders from governing bodies across the world towards this rising concern – the concern of building the capability of organizations and nations for workforce reskilling on an ongoing basis. It is also an attempt to bring forth the unearthed potential of 'self-skilling', that can be leveraged as an effective tool for reskilling. The book brings a new and essential dimension to Human Resource Management for Industry 5.0, which is the aspect of reskilling, keeping people relevant, and saving them from becoming redundant in the world of work.

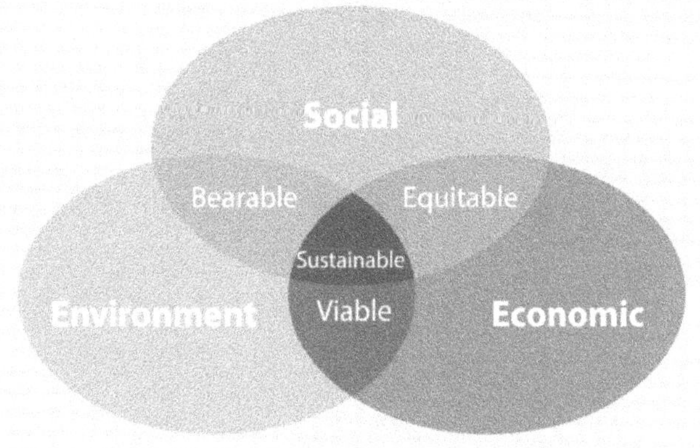

Figure 1.1: Scheme of Sustainable Development

Source: https://en.wikipedia.org/wiki/Equity_(economics)

PART I

Great Skills Disruption and the Reskilling Revolution

CHAPTER – 1

COVID-19 and the High-Stakes Game of Automation

Picture yourself standing at a fork in the road. On one path, we are drawn toward a future straight out of science fiction with mind-blowing advancements in technology like cloud computing, Artificial Intelligence (AI), and the Internet of Things (IOT). But there is a catch – these very innovations pose a threat by potentially wiping out countless jobs as machines become smarter and more capable.

This is not just some made-up scenario; it is happening right now. Yes, we do see a bunch of new jobs emerging, but they are nothing like what our parents knew. They require a whole new set of skills, ones we did not learn in school or college. So, while some people are seizing these opportunities, others are left feeling lost and unsure of how to adapt.

Just when we thought we were getting the hang of this high-tech world, the COVID-19 pandemic acted like a fast-forward button, hurling us into an era, where going digital is no longer optional – it is downright essential. But It is like being handed a powerful new tool to deal with the disruption, with little guidance on how to use it without getting hurt.

This is a collective challenge, no doubt about it. We are talking about reshaping whole industries and redefining the nature of work itself. Whether you are an individual, a business owner, or a policy maker, you have got your skin in this game. The question now is, how are we all going to navigate this complex landscape without leaving anyone behind?

Fortunately, we have access to more resources now than ever before. From online tutorials and educational materials to digital coaching services and group workshops, there are countless ways we can gain the necessary skills to adjust our approach to this new reality. And with so many technology-based tools and alternatives in the market, it has never been easier to find a solution that fits anyone's specific individual needs.

Just as we were trying to wrap our heads around this whirlwind of change, along came the COVID-19 pandemic, acting like a turbocharger on an already roaring engine. Far from slowing down the technological transformation, the pandemic has put it into overdrive.

Imagine, millions of jobs, gone in a flash, as machines take over tasks we used to do. But at the same time, almost 100 million new jobs are forming, custom-built for this brave new world where people and machines share the stage.

The catch here is that we do not have years to adapt. According to the experts at the World Economic Forum, 40% of us need new skills, and fast, just to stay in the game. We are talking about something like a crash course that lasts six months or less and trains us for these new jobs . Employers are catching on too; they have kicked their expectations up a notch, by now demanding that virtually all their workers learn on the fly. Now this is a big jump from just a few years ago, when learning to do a new job was more systematic, planned, and generously paced in one's professional journey.

But even if you are one of the lucky ones who gets to keep your job, don't get too comfortable. The skillset you relied on yesterday, about 40% of that is on the chopping block, and is set to be replaced or revamped.

Now this is not all of it. In addition to the risk of unemployment staring at those who are employed today, we also have over 200 million people globally who already can't find work. According to a projection from the International Labor Organization, we are staring down a shortage of 52 million full-time jobs, and every day that passes, makes a bounce-back seem like a pipe dream.

This is a tightrope we are walking, and there is no safety net. Job markets are contracting, opportunities are vanishing, and the clock is ticking for workers everywhere to rewrite their own scripts.

Imagine a serene, steady descent down a mountain, each year feeling a little lighter, a little more hopeful. This was the global unemployment story from 2010 to 2019 with a steady growth in jobs and employment across all industry sectors. Then, just as we were about to reach the base, we were jolted off course. Instead of the anticipated smooth sail, 2020 thrusts us into a dizzying climb. Unemployment didn't just rise, it rocketed in a flash and a staggering 37.72 million people, once employed, suddenly found themselves adrift.

This was not some random twist of fate or an act of nature – at least not entirely. COVID-19, the ultimate disruptor got countries worldwide locked down, taking a rain check on the economy and sealing millions away from their jobs. Like a universal pause button, except when played again, the tune was entirely different.

And while we were still reeling from that unexpected blow, the world was already morphing, with technology steering the ship. AI and Automation, long the domain of industry reports on "Future of Work" , was suddenly a very tangible reality. Digital solutions were not just "nice to have" anymore, they were the gold standard.

This tech evolution, combined with the pandemic's pressure, did not paint every industry with the same brush. The hospitality world, with its bustling restaurants and vibrant hotels, suddenly discovered that almost half of its core could vanish. While, on the other end, professionals in government, finance, and certain sectors found themselves on a more stable ground, with risks limited to a much more manageable 2% to 8% of their workforce.

The low-wage worker, often on the front lines, the backbone of many industries, faced a disproportionate upheaval. They were not just sidelined but were often completely removed from the game.

Welcome to the Dawn of Tomorrow's Work

In the sprawling saga of industries yet to unfold, six behemoths cast a towering shadow: Cloud computing, big data, e-commerce, the arcane world of encryption, robots without a human grin, and the mind of tomorrow, artificial intelligence. These titans are the very sculptors of our professional tomorrow. .

As businesses rally behind these six giants, almost 55% enterprises state that they are redesigning the composition of the value chain in their business. With emerging workforce strategies, the dance between man and machine gets a fresh choreography. It is not merely a tale of machines doing more and the share of man versus machine tasks, it is the entire stage transforming. On one hand, an eye-opening 43% of enterprises, predict a trimming of their human ensemble, while on the other hand,34% have plans to expand their workforce owing to deeper technological integration. Increased hiring of contractors for task specialized work is another predicted change in the organizational workforce strategy.

Certain tasks of yesteryear workspace like digging up information, data processing, and administration are being handed off to the silent, meticulous machines. It is not about sidelining the human spirit; it is about changing the players. Still, there are roles where our essence as humans cannot be muted. Jobs demanding decisions instilled with wisdom, the connective tissue of communication, clear-eyed reasoning, and the age-old art of management. These are not somethings one can program; these are uniquely, and undeniably human.

Zoom into near future. the horizon promises more than just a shift; it heralds a revolution. Machines, with their razor-sharp precision, are staking their claim, especially in the realms of data, the competitive arena of job hunts, the brave world of technology, and the raw mechanics of manual labour. But when the game is about human connections – the very act of talking, deciding, and leading – our role is untouchable. The machines are gaining ground, but it certainly is not game over for us.

Globally, there are a staggering 85 million jobs predicted to be displaced by 2025. This will result in millions of workers vanishing from organizations just like characters ending the part of their roles in a story. At the same time, another breathtaking 97 million new jobs are expected to be added into the industries. As these jobs unfold, they are ready to redefine the script, they are setting the stage for the next epic saga in the industrial world.

If the World Economic Forum's "Jobs of Tomorrow" report were a movie trailer, you would feel the pulse of a dramatic blockbuster in the making. A riveting cast of 99 job roles is ready to grab the limelight across major world stages, as they get identified as the most in demand jobs. Besides the AI enthusiasts, the digital daredevils, and the robotic stars, these include a diverse array of specialist roles emerging in each industry sector.

Materials engineers sculpting tomorrow's rides in the automotive sector, e-commerce experts and social media entrepreneurs capture the digital stage in the consumer space industry, renewable energy innovators in the energy sector, Fintech futurists in the financial services, biologists and geneticists in the healthcare sector, and remote sensing experts in mining and metal, weave technology threads into the core fabric of the industry.

The scales are shifting, and the skill set menu is getting a modern revamp. We are not just in a new chapter; It is a whole new book. Automation is not just handing out new roles; it is reshuffling the entire deck of job roles across industries. It is a grand strategy game, where entire sectors and roles are making calculated moves. Some roles are fading into the shadows, while others are ascending to the forefront. The ripples of this are far-reaching and profound. It is not just about the job titles; it is about their volume, their place of honour, and the value we attach to them.

As machines step in, elbowing out routine, methodical tasks, they inadvertently cast a spotlight on the unique strengths of the human spirit. Those mundane tasks machines can replicate are just the tip of the iceberg. Beneath the surface, there is a treasure trove of skills that only humans can truly master: problem-solving, leadership, and the art of emotional intelligence. In this reshaped job landscape, our innate abilities to create, innovate, and empathize are not just nice to have – they are invaluable.

McKinsey Global provides a fascinating snapshot. Using O*NET data, they delved deep, analysing over 2,000 work activities across 800+ occupations from 2020. Breaking down skills into categories like Physical, Cognitive, Social-Emotional, and Technological, they painted a picture of the current industrial landscape.

The findings are clear as day. To glide seamlessly into higher-wage occupations – roles that promise both quality and longevity – workers need to arm themselves with a blend of technological prowess and the irreplaceable social-emotional toolkit.

The Skill Spectrum: Charting the Landscape of Tomorrow

Step into the daily grind of today's worker. Their landscape is a puzzle, each piece marked by distinct roles and responsibilities, shaped by their position on the wage ladder. Down at the foundation, you are ankle-deep in manual tasks, claiming 50% of your time, as Figure 1.2 vividly sketches. about 18% of your time where you are using some basic cognitive skills, about 13% in decision-making and analysis, 15% of your time when you are using your emotional and social skills and merely 5% of your time you are using technological skills.

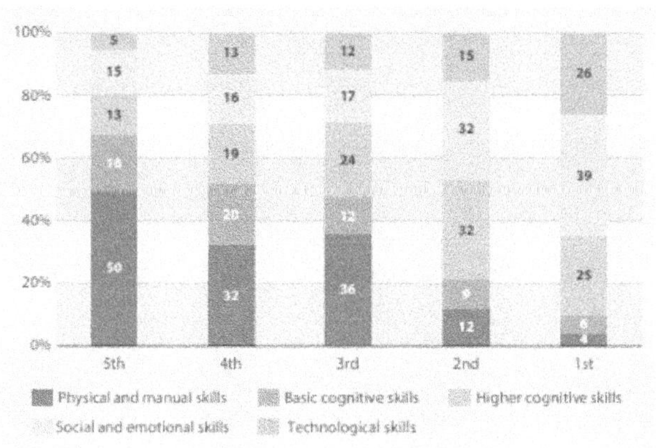

Figure 1.2 Skills for Occupational Transitions to Better Quality Jobs
Source: Lund et al., 2021

Now, let us change the altitude. You are higher up, breathing in the crisp air of the wage spectrum's zenith. The terrain transforms. Manual tasks have shrunk to a mere 4% footprint. Basic cognition to just 6%, but higher cognitive skills dominating at 25% alongside emotional intelligence at a significant 39% and technology prowess at 26%.

Mercer's 2021 Future Skills Survey Report is less of a report, more of a survival guide. Adaptability is not just a trait; it is your North Star. Pair it with a growth mindset, and you've got your survival toolkit in this new world of work.

In today's professional landscape, some patches appear less solid than others. Those once-sturdy fields of administration, HR, and data entry are showing cracks, inching towards a cliff, thanks to the relentless march of automation. If Mercer's whispers hold truth, these might be the initial domains to feel innovation's remodelling touch.

We are in the heart of a metamorphic era. It feels like standing on a giant conveyor belt, ever in motion. The once-sacred concept of the office and its boundaries are shattered. Its scope is now as boundless as the horizon. COVID-19 didn't just teach us, it reshaped our workspaces – from cozy corners of our homes to sunlit park benches and the ambient hum of cafes across continents. Health and safety didn't just draw a line; they sketched an entirely new canvas of work, peppered with pixels and diversity.

Post this health turmoil, a tech wave surged, engulfing enterprises in its wake. Every heartbeat, every fleeting moment, echoes with the rhythm of automation and the hum of remote collaborations. Sure, job terrains felt the initial tremors, jolted by upheavals. But peer past the immediate gloom of unemployment shadows, and a glint catches the eye: technology, in its grand design, might just be a net job creator in the coming years like it has always in the past industrial evolutions.

In boardrooms and policy chambers, a rallying cry resonates – 'reskill and upskill'. It is less a suggestion and more the anthem of our age. Multiple deep dives into data sing a similar tune: investing in skills is no mere cost. It is the cornerstone, the keystone of a bridge connecting businesses to the broader fabric of society. This journey is not just about riding the waves; it is about charting new waters. Each reskilled individual is not just a statistic; they are the forerunners of a transformative movement – sometimes within sectors, often bridging them.

McKinsey's 2021 crystal ball shows Remote Work, Digitalization, and Automation reshaping our occupational DNA by 2030. The numbers predict seismic shifts. We are talking about a colossal 72 million workers from just China and India – diving into new occupational waters. There is an recede in demand for roles like office support and customer service. However, the tides rise favourably for STEM workers, health professionals, and wellness enthusiasts, among others.

Figure 1.3 unfolds the job transition narrative: professionals are not just adapting, they are metamorphosing. Amidst this evolving jobscape, while many have found solace in burgeoning roles, others have boldly charted into unexplored territories, making grand occupational leaps.

What is the compass guiding these shifts? The skill profiles are inherent to each occupation. Blend these with the attractiveness of prospective job destinations, and there you are! Figures 1.3 and 1.4 show how affected workers are transitioning into new occupations.

Yet, as we steer through the post-COVID-19 world, the number steering towards uncharted occupational territories might swell, as hinted by Figure 1.3. To decipher what an 'occupational transition' truly means – imagine a role being washed away by time's tide, never to return, even as the demand for labour surges.

Flip back in time to the pre-COVID-19 world illustrated in Figure 1.3. Picture it as a vast mural painted with eight distinct trends: automation's rise, ballooning incomes, greying populations, technology's march, the looming shadow of climate change, infrastructural revolutions, soaring education levels, and the newfound worth of unpaid work.

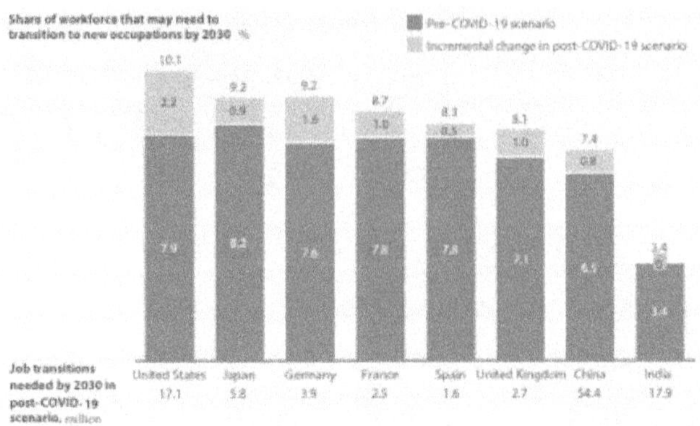

Figure 1.3 Transitions of Affected Professionals
Source: Lund et al., 2021

Fast forward to a post-COVID-19 tableau, and the canvas becomes more intricate. Beyond the original eight, new brush strokes emerge, painting tales of swift automation, burgeoning e-commerce, the surge of remote work, and a shrinking footprint of business travel.

These shifts are not mere ripples but tidal waves, prompting many more across the globe to embark on new occupational voyages. And while countries like China and India might seem more resilient to these post-pandemic effects, delve deeper, and the sheer magnitude is astounding. Just fathom this: a combined force of over 72 million workers from just these two nations, venturing into the brave new world of fresh occupations.

Charting New Professional Horizons

Figure 1.4, unfolds an intricate map of career reinventions. For those with the audacity to re-route their professional journeys, the expanse is vast and the pathways varied. A closer inspection reveals fascinating trajectories: a remarkable 72% of pioneers in the Data and AI sector have ventured from entirely different career landscapes. The fields of product development welcome a diverse influx, while the realm of people and culture predominantly attracts talents from the HR domain. Meanwhile, engineering and people-focused roles pull in 19% and 26% of their workforce, respectively, from diverse backgrounds. Such profound shifts in skill landscapes pave myriad avenues for those willing to traverse new paths.

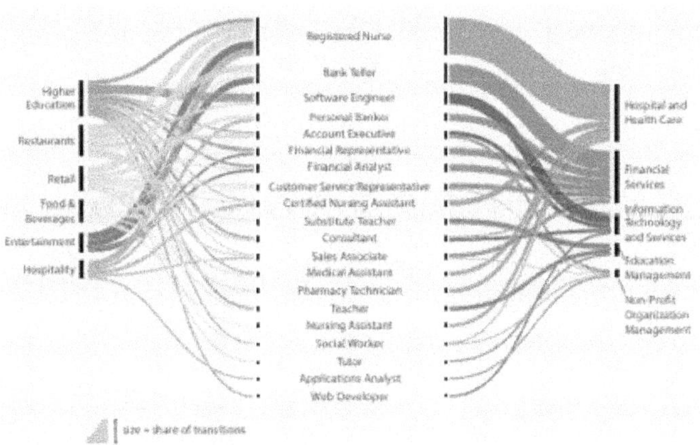

Figure 1.4: *In Focus Transitions for Affected Professionals*

Source: Forum, 2020

Armed with the right toolkit for reskilling and upskilling, many can pinpoint their next destination. It is noteworthy that businesses, perceiving the transformative trends, are extending bridges of opportunity. An encouraging 62% of employees are walking these bridges, with plans to invite another 11% by 2025. Yet, the challenge remains: only 42% have truly embarked on this enlightening journey.

To navigate these dynamic pathways, one does not need an exhaustive roadmap. However, proficiency in key skills ensures fewer detours. Industry leaders now prioritize attributes like analytical thinking, adaptability, resilience, and fervour for active learning as key markers on this journey.

The Renaissance of Reskilling

The world is on fast-forward, where the winds of change don't just whisper, they roar. It is an era where the ability to shift, morph, and evolve isn't just a luxury – it is the very bedrock of survival. However, a formidable barrier emerges for many – the shackles of debt, the weight of student loans, or the golden handcuffs of specialized job benefits. It is like being in a race with an anchor tied to your feet, feeling the pulse of progress but being held back.

So, what is the remedy to this siren's call of stagnation? The antidote lies in fostering flexibility and nurturing growth. While there is a silver lining, with many finding their niche in emerging industries, merely stepping into these arenas is not enough. It is about sprinting, jumping hurdles, and consistently levelling up.

Another new reality is that an astonishing 94% of employers are no longer just directing their teams; they are cheering them on to craft their own paths, polish their skills, to shine brighter with each passing day. The current playbook is a digital tune, with organizations taking the reins of their team's evolution. The message they are broadcasting is unambiguous: in this chapter of our collective journey, self-direction and ceaseless learning are the heroes of the tale.

The Confluence of COVID-19 and Automation Across Industries

In the aftermath of COVID-19, global industries are in a state of flux, their trajectories recalibrated by the relentless march of automation. Diving deep into the details, as captured in Table 1.1, we get a front-row seat to the prevailing trends sculpting tomorrow.

An alarming 15% of the world's working brigade stands on the precipice of obsolescence. Yet, every storm has its rainbow: an optimistic 45% reintegration rate beckons those affected. Yet, it is not a monolithic march. Some domains, like Education and Government, find the path to reintegration more complicated, echoing the distinctive challenges each industry houses.

The automotive realm is a striking case in point. Here, the ripples of skills instability make towering waves. Zooming out for a more expansive perspective, this unease touches a significant 43% across the spectrum, sounding an unmistakable call for resilience, adaptability, and perpetual learning. Meanwhile, in the corridors of technology, cloud computing reigns supreme, acting as a beacon guiding industries through tumultuous seas. With this shift towards a tech-dominant horizon, the blueprint for professional success is being redrawn. Active learning, intertwined with a forward-thinking mindset, is increasingly becoming the golden ticket in this reshaped arena. And thanks to the pandemic, the march towards digitization has only quickened its pace, compelling employees to become digital natives.

When we focus the lens on job roles, data analysts and scientists emerge as the poster children of this renewed work ecosystem. On the flip side, loyalists of yesteryears, like data entry clerks, find themselves on shaky ground. There is a clear alarm ringing for approximately 56% of businesses: a significant skills chasm that stands tall, especially as they flirt with cutting-edge technologies.

Now, automation is a double-edged sword. It promises unparalleled efficiencies but simultaneously stokes fears of job cuts. And the stats echo this sentiment – nearly half, or 47% of companies, are giving a nod to potential downsizing driven by automation. Yet, some sectors, including IT, Education, Government, and professional services, seem to be donning armour, showing resilience against immediate workforce shrinkages.

Reskilling is the order of the day. A focus on analytical thinking and innovation is palpable, as companies prioritize these areas in their upskilling initiatives. The division of labour between humans and machines is increasingly clear-cut, with machines dominating tasks related to information and data processing. In contrast, roles centred around coordination, advising, and management remain the stronghold of the human workforce. The reskilling trajectory varies in duration. A promising 26% of the global workforce is poised to adapt within a month. Yet, the majority face longer timelines: 21% envision a 1–3-month journey, 18% anticipate 3–6 months, 17% project 6–12 months, and 19%, the path extends beyond a year.

As we stand at the crossroads of a post-COVID-19 world, one thing is abundantly clear: change is the only constant. The relentless march of automation, juxtaposed with the unprecedented upheavals of the pandemic, has reshaped the contours of the global workforce.

The figures and trends captured herein underscore the need for adaptability and resilience. From the rise of remote work and flow of occupational transitions, our approach to work is being redefined. The necessity for upskilling and reskilling emerges as a trumpet call to both individuals and organizations, ensuring that the human element remains at the heart of our ever-evolving digital era.

However, it is not solely about metrics and patterns. It is also about our capacity to adapt in the face of obstacles and the collaborative duty of building a future where technology enhances, rather than replaces, human potential.

Table 1.1: *Industry Profiles and Re-skilling Needs*

Source: J. Brown et al., 2017; Forum, 2020; Lund et al., 2021

	Industry Profiles													Average reskilling needs (share of workforce within the industry)				
Industry	Avg share of workers at risk of displacement	Expected redeployment success rate of displaced workers	Avg skills instability among workforce	Top Technology adoption	Top emerging skill	Top Covid-19 impact on company strategy	Top emerging Job Role	Top Redundant Job Role	Skill gaps in local labour market as a barrier to adoption of new technologies	Companies to Reduce current workforce due to automation	Top Reskilling area	Job task with top machine share	Job task with top human share	less than 1 month	1-3 months	3-6 months	6-12 months	over 1 year
Advanced Manufacturing	14%	41.30%	43.60%	Cloud computing	Technology use, monitoring and control	Accelerate digitalization of work processes	Business Development Professionals	Assembly and Factory workers	67.70%	45.20%	Technology use, monitoring and con-trol	Information and data processing	Reasoning and decision making	26.80%	22.40%	16.60%	20.60%	13.60%
Agriculture, Food & Beverage	11.20%	47.60%	35.80%	IOT and connected devices	Active learning and learning strategies	Accelerate digitalization of work processes	Data analysts and scientists	Data entry clerks	52.90%	41.20%	Leadership and social influence	Information and data processing	Coordinating, developing, managing and advising	38.60%	20.80%	21.10%	6.80%	12.80%
Automotive	19.10%	44.40%	55.20%	Big Data Analytics	Analytical thinking and innovation	Accelerate digitalization of work processes	Data analysts and scientists	Data entry clerks	50%	61.10%	Analyt-ical thinking and innovation	Information and data processing	Coordinating, developing, managing and advising	31.20%	22.20%	16.40%	14.10%	16.10%

	Industry Profiles													Average reskilling needs (share of workforce within the industry)				
Industry	Avg share of workers at risk of displacement	Expected redeployment success rate of displaced workers	Avg skills instability among workforce	Top Technology adoption	Top emerging skill	Top Covid-19 impact on company strategy	Top emerging Job Role	Top Redundant Job Role	Skill gaps in local labour market as a barrier to adoption of new technologies	Companies to Reduce current workforce due to automation	Top Reskilling area	Job task with top machine share	Job task with top human share	less than 1 month	1-3 months	3-6 months	6-12 months	over 1 year
Consumer	16.80%	49.90%	43.20%	IOT and connected devices	Complex Problem Solving	Provide more opportunities to work remotely	Data analysts and scientists	Data entry clerks	48.50%	32.40%	Active learning and learning strategies	Information and data processing	Coordinating, develo-ping, managing and advising	24%	26.90%	22.40%	12.50%	14.20%
Information Technology	17.50%	49.40%	44.10%	Cloud computing	Analytical thinking and innovation	Accelerate digitalization of work processes	AI and machine learning specialists	Data entry clerks	60%	-	Analytical thinking and innovation	Information and data processing	Coordinating, developing, managing and advising	26.20%	19.70%	19.30%	16.10%	18.70%
Education	13.90%	30.90%	41.30%	Cloud computing	Creativity, originality and initiative	Accelerate digitalization of work processes	Vocational, Univer-sity Higher Educa-tion Teachers	Administrative and executive secretaries	45.50%	-	Analytical thinking and innovation	Information and data processing	Reasoning and decision making	25.20%	24.50%	17.20%	12.20%	20.90%

	Industry Profiles												Average reskilling needs (share of workforce within the industry)				
Industry	Avg share of workers at risk of displacement	Expected redeployment success rate of displaced workers	Avg skills instability among workforce	Top Technology adoption	Top emerging skill	Top Covid-19 impact on company strategy	Top emerging Job Role	Top Redundant Job Role	Skill gaps in local labour market as a barrier to adoption of new technologies	Companies to Reduce current workforce due to automation	Top Reskilling area	Job task with top machine share	Job task with top human share	less than 1 month	1-3 months	3-6 months	6-12 months	over 1 year
Energy & Utilities	11.80%	51.10%	39.40%	IOT and connected devices	Critical thinking and analysis	Accelerate digitalization of work processes	Data analysts and scientists	Administrative and executive secretaries	70.60%	29.40%	Critical thinking and analysis	Information and data processing	Reasoning and decision making	24%	17.50%	14.40%	12.80%	31.40%
Financial Services	20.80%	50.50%	44.10%	Cloud computing	Analytical thinking and innovation	Accelerate digitalization of work processes	Data analysts and scientists	Data entry clerks	58.50%	50%	Leadership and social influence	Information and data processing	Coordinating, developing, managing and advising	26.90%	17.10%	13.40%	19.80%	22.90%
Government & Public Sector	14.80%	39.50%	39.10%	Encryption and cyber security	Leadership and social influence	Provide more opportunities to work remotely	Information security analysts	Accounting, Bookkeeping and payroll clerks	50%	-	Analytical thinking and innovation	Information and data processing	Coordinating, developing, managing and advising	27.30%	24.90%	15.90%	21.80%	10.10%

	Industry Profiles													Average reskilling needs (share of workforce within the industry)				
Industry	Avg share of workers at risk of displace-ment	Expected redeploy-ment success rate of displaced workers	Avg skills instabi-lity among work-force	Top Tech-nology adoption	Top emerg-ing skill	Top Covid-19 impact on company strategy	Top emerging Job Role	Top Redun-dant Job Role	Skill gaps in local labour market as a barrier to adoption of new technolo-gies	Compa-nies to Reduce current work-force due to automa-tion	Top Reskill-ing area	Job task with top machine share	Job task with top human share	less than 1 month	1-3 months	3-6 months	6-12 months	over 1 year
Health-care	10.60%	44.20%	48.20%	IOT and connec-ted devices	Active learn-ing and learning strate-gies	Provide more opportu-nities to work remotely	Data analy-sts and scien-tists	Data entry clerks	42.10%	63.20%	Creati-vity, origina-lity and initia-tive	Informa-tion and data proess-ing	Comm-unicating and inter-acting	22.30%	23.20%	21.50%	25.20%	7.80%
Manu-facturing	13.20%	44.60%	43.60%	Cloud compu-ting	Active learn-ing and learn-ing strate-gies	Provide more opport-unities to work remotely	Data analy-sts and scien-tists	Admini-strative and execu-tive secreta-ries	63.60%	50%	Analyti-cal think-ing and innova-tion	Informa-tion and data process-ing	Reason-ing and deci-sion making	23.80%	22.40%	19.40%	16.50%	17.90%

	Industry Profiles													Average reskilling needs (share of workforce within the industry)				
Industry	Avg share of workers at risk of displace-ment	Expected redeploy-ment success rate of displaced workers	Avg skills instabi-lity among work-force	Top Tech-nology adoption	Top emerg-ing skill	Top Covid-19 impact on company strategy	Top emerg-ing Job Role	Top Redun-dant Job Role	Skill gaps in local labour market as a barrier to adoption of new technolo-gies	Compa-nies to Reduce current work-force due to automa-tion	Top Reskill-ing area	Job task with top machine share	Job task with top human share	less than 1 month	1-3 months	3-6 months	6-12 months	over 1 year
Mining and Metals	19.90%	49.50%	40.60%	Robots, non human-oid (drones, indus-trial automa-tion etc.)	Techno-logy use, moni-toring and control	Provide more opport-unities to work remotely	AI and machine learning specia-lists	Data entry clerks	73.30%	51.70%	Analy-tical think-ing and innova-tion	Informa-tion and data process-ing	Coordina-ting, develo-ping, manag-ing and advis-ing	17.50%	22.70%	15.60%	19.50%	24.70%
Oil & Gas	14.20%	48.10%	42.60%	IOT and connec-ted devices	Active learn-ing and learning strate-gies	Acceler-ate digitali-zation of work proces-ses	Renew-able Energy Engi-neers	Admini-strative and execu-tive secreta-ries	50%	42.90%	Tech-nology design and program-ming	Informa-tion and data process-ing	Reason-ing and deci-sion making	13.60%	16.10%	22.40%	19.90%	28.10%

	Industry Profiles													Average reskilling needs (share of workforce within the industry)				
Industry	Avg share of workers at risk of displacement	Expected redeployment success rate of displaced workers	Avg skills instability among workforce	Top Technology adoption	Top emerging skill	Top Covid-19 impact on company strategy	Top emerging Job Role	Top Redundant Job Role	Skill gaps in local labour market as a barrier to adoption of new technologies	Companies to Reduce current workforce due to automation	Top Reskilling area	Job task with top machine share	Job task with top human share	less than 1 month	1-3 months	3-6 months	6-12 months	over 1 year
Professional Services	11.60%	41.30%	48%	Cloud computing	Analytical thinking and innovation	Accelerate digitalization of work proces-ses	Digital Marketing and strategy specialists	Administrative and executive secretaries	41.20%	-	Active learning and learning strategies	Looking for and receiving job related information	Reason-ing and decision making	29%	20.50%	17.10%	15.60%	17.80%
Transporation and Storage	14.70%	49.10%	38.20%	Big Data Analytics	Active learn-ing and learn-ing strategies	Accelerate digitalization of work proces-ses	AI and machine learning specialists	Administrative and executive secretaries	64.70%	47.10%	Analytical thinking and innovation	Information and data processing	Coordinating, deve-loping, manag-ing and advising	26.60%	14.40%	16%	16.10%	26.80%
Overall	15%	45%	43%	Cloud computing	Active learning and learning strategies	Accelerate digitalization of work proces-ses	Data analysts and scientists	Data entry clerks	56%	47%	Analytical think-ing and innovation	Information and data processing	Coordinating, developing, managing and advising	26%	21%	18%	17%	19%

CHAPTER – 2

Re-skilling and Upskilling: An Indian Perspective

Imagine standing on the bustling streets of Mumbai or the serene banks of the Ganges. No matter where you look, India is brimming with potential. With its staggering working age population of 588,373,756, and more than half of them actively participating in the workforce, it is evident that this nation is not just waiting for the future – it is shaping it.

Even though nearly half of this hardworking population is digitally savvy, there is a disconnect. The WEF report suggests that while the drive and ambition are there, the skill fulfilment is not catching up fast enough. And, well, about three-quarters of these hardworking folks are in a precarious balancing act, tiptoeing on the edge of uncertain job scenarios. The numbers don't lie: India's workforce needs a reskilling revolution, and it is high time.

Peeking into the heart of India's technology landscape, is like witnessing a dance of progression. Most Indian enterprises, almost a whopping 98% of them, are riding the cloud wave, reshaping how business is done.

Encryption and Cybersecurity is another set of technologies reshaping Indian organizations. 95% of firms are ensuring their digital territories remain unbreached. The Internet of Things is not a futuristic concept anymore, it is a reality for 90% of Indian enterprises, intertwining their operations into a seamless weave.

Use of Big data analytics, an 88% commitment means businesses are not just making decisions – they are predicting the future. Almost 86% of firms are refining user interactions using natural language processing technologies. AI and Machine Learning ensemble are boasting an 81% adoption across Indian firms.

Standing at the heart of this India, we are surrounded by a technology landscape that is rapidly changing. Besides the above, almost 75% firms in India are adopting non-humanoid robots, and blockchain dynamics . E-commerce and digital trade platforms come alive, offering a shopping spree like never before. Almost 64% firms are adopting new age power storage and generation technologies.

Yet, amid this sprawling technological panorama, there is a sense of urgency. India, with all its potential, stands at a crossroads. The direction it takes will shape its global standing. Ensuring that this transformative potential turns into real-world success hinges on effectively upskilling its massive workforce. It is a collective effort, requiring strategic policies, industry drive, and the burning ambition of countless individuals.

In the post-COVID era, and India seems reborn, much like a phoenix. There is a palpable shift in the air; businesses have adjusted their sails to navigate the new normal. If you were to eavesdrop on the corporate chatter, you would hear tales of a monumental shift towards remote work, with an astounding 90% of companies rallying behind it.

Digitization is no longer just a buzzword from days gone by. It is the roaring anthem, with a staggering 87% of companies building strategies for adoption of automation . More than half of the corporate sphere seems ready to embrace digitization and automation, eyeing a future where efficiency reigns and errors fade into oblivion.

Over half of the expansive corporate terrain in India, is not just adjusting their strategy but placing reskilling and upskilling at the very heart of their vision. This shift is echoing India's unyielding commitment to progress and adaptability in a world turned upside down.

The conversations in the plush conference rooms are not with just plans and projections, but with dreams. Dreams of cultivating a workforce that does not just work but thinks, innovates, and leads. Analytical sharpness, a flair for innovation, and a tenacity for growth are essentials. But that is not all. The rooms resonate with discussions about fostering leaders, influencers, and gifted individuals who can gaze upon chaos and find clarity.

A technology team's discourse, on the other hand, is not about mere tech solutions but a deep understanding of design, intricacies, and the heartbeat of the digital age. Yet, amidst this cascade of skills, three words shimmer brightly: resilience, stress tolerance, and flexibility. It is as if they are the new guardians, ready to steer India's corporate ship through stormy seas. And as one would anchor a ship safely, the importance of quality control and safety vigilance is not just noted; it is revered, a fitting close to the skillset of tomorrow's champions.

Emerging Skills in India

Walking through the bustling corridors of an modern Indian tech hub, you breathe in the atmosphere that pulsates with a palpable energy – the kind that speaks of dreams being crafted and horizons being expanded. And right in the middle of all this are individuals with a razor-sharp analytical mind and an inventive spirit. They are not just the analysts or tech whizzes; they are the modern-day wizards of our age, conjuring solutions, and innovations at every turn.

On one side we can visualize, there is the suave AI expert, who converses as comfortably with machines as with humans. Not too far away, a data analyst pores over screens, extracting stories and insights from strings of numbers. There is the security guru, always alert, guarding the digital fortresses, while IoT enthusiasts sketch out interconnected futures. And don't miss the big data specialists, project maestros, fintech mavericks, and digital marketers – the vanguards, sculpting India's tomorrow.

But as we drift further down these corridors, there is a different scene. Rooms once abuzz with administrative chatter seem quieter. The assembly lines, which roared with activity, echo a softer hum. Managerial cabins are evolving, and reshaping. Traditional roles, once the bedrock of businesses, now seem like relics in a museum – a testament to a bygone era. It is like watching the tides of time, sweeping some ahead while leaving others to adapt or recede.

Projected Use of Training Providers

At the heart of the bustling marketplace, 41.5% of India's firms are collaborating closely with their in-housetraining specialists. This is not just about leaning on familiar shoulders; it is about harnessing home-grown expertise to craft strategies that resonate deeply within their own walls.

Almost 21.1% of the firms are not just browsing but actively engaging with the global digital caravans who specialize in online training. These are not casual conversations; they are a series of deep dives into vast oceans of digital knowledge, embracing the future of learning with both hands.

Private academies with their alluring facades cater to 17.7% of firms. They do not just offer courses; they offer curated experiences, blending niche knowledge with tailored techniques, inviting firms into an intimate dance of learning.

Yet, amidst this mosaic of modernity, the grand old libraries stand resilient. The traditional seats of learning — public and private institutions, flanked by public training centres — might hold a smaller space, but their influence is profound. They are the sentinels of time-tested wisdom, ensuring that as the nation strides forward, it does so with a reverent nod to its roots. There is a profound realization here. As India's corporate entities navigate this diverse educational landscape, the journey is both a celebration of what is new and a tribute to the timeless.

India, with its vast populace and storied legacy as a global talent provider, finds itself at a unique crossroads. The challenges before it loom large, yet so do the opportunities. It is not merely about cultivating the prowess that thrives within its vast boundaries; it is a story that has implications far and wide. Addressing India's reskilling challenge is not a solitary endeavour but a global commitment. In this unfolding saga of progress and innovation, India's steps are not just felt locally. The world watches, participates, and relies on its every move.

"The world is undergoing a reskilling revolution. Alongside the need for protecting millions of people from unemployment due to changes in the job landscape, we are also entering a new era that calls for embracing lifelong learning and reskilling as a way of life."

PART II

Understanding Reskilling & Related Subject Areas

CHAPTER – 3

Reskilling Research

For years academic researchers have adopted systematic and scientific approaches to explore and create a body of knowledge that help us in developing a better understanding of various aspects of the world we live in. It is this large scale systematic collaboration for continuously learning from experience and exploration that enables progress and evolution for humanity. When we delve into reskilling research, various academic disciplines unfurl, each casting its own intricate shadow. Social sciences, psychology, information technology, and management, each discipline weaves its own narrative, painting a vivid panorama of the reskilling phenomenon.

Concepts of self-directed learning, eLearning, mLearning, skill acquisition, and skill development, explain the harmonious symphony of reskilling and lifelong learning emerging in the modern workplace. The most popular models, theories, and constructs known to academia help understand this phenomenon as workplaces of tomorrow evolve.

For the custodians of management research, this chapter is not merely ink on paper, it is akin to a beacon in the night, illuminating the intricate pathways of reskilling research. It presents the essence of reskilling and its kindred spirits—domains like Self-Directed Learning and Workplace Learning meticulously charted through a bibliometric analysis. Six pillars of research emerge, each echoing its own discovery, and innovation that help decode the phenomena of reskilling and lifelong learning. The reverberations shape our narrative, offering both depth and direction to our understanding.

Reskilling: The Ascending Arc

In academic research, the area of Reskilling had a quiet beginning in 1981, its voice was barely a whisper for decades. In 2018, a crescendo began, with an explosion of insights and explorations that has not ceased yet. This once-muted topic now holds a fever pitch, resonating across academic halls and boardrooms alike.

The United States and the United Kingdom lead the charge globally, blazing trails and setting benchmarks in reskilling research. South Africa and Australia, too, are more than mere bystanders, lending their own rich perspectives. Placed at the fifth spot, is India — not just participating, but shaping the dialogue. And while globally, the corpus of Reskilling literature might seem modest, with a mere 293 published research papers in the popular research database-Scopus, India's enthusiasm is evident, staking its claim as a front-runner by being amongst the top 10 countries where researchers are exploring the subject aggressively.

Self-Directed Learning: A Tale of Two Pathways

The second pillar of research associated with reskilling traces back to 1956, when the archives of Self-directed learning (SDL) research began to weave a story picking pace as the eighties dawned. Interestingly, just as SDL research had to erupt in scholarly fervour, a sibling area branched out with emergence of eLearning The progress in SDL research in subsequent years was significant yet was overshadowed by the meteoric rise of eLearning as an area of interest among researchers. While both topics are cut from the same cloth, their trajectories in the academic world have been markedly distinct, offering a rich tableau of progress, evolution, and transformation.

Just like Reskilling, a diverse ensemble of nations is sculpting the discourse in SDL research too. The United States stands tall, closely followed by other luminaries like the UK, Canada, and Australia casting their own formidable glow, enriching the SDL literature. From South Korea's modern academies to Germany's traditional halls, from the innovative labs of the Netherlands and China to the bustling campuses of Taiwan, the story of self-directed learning unfolds. And as these narrative weaves its way through diverse geographies, India too adds its threads, securing a noteworthy tenth spot on the global stage of SDL research.

eLearning: The Digital Dawn

From the fertile grounds of Self-Directed Learning sprouted two tech-savvy offshoots: eLearning and mLearning. The new millennium was their playground, and their ascent, post-2000, has been nothing short of spectacular. In the vast academic repository that is the Scopus database, they shine with a staggering collection, with eLearning amassing over 92,000 published research papers.

The eLearning and mLearning knowledge landscape is a testament to global collaboration. The United States and China, in their tech-driven avatars, lead this digital renaissance. But this is not a duet. The UK's scholarly fervor, Spain's innovative strides, Germany's meticulous methodologies, Australia's forward-thinking approaches, Taiwan's tech-first initiatives, Japan's precision, and Italy's creative inputs — all harmonize and reflect in the rich literature created by researchers of these countries on the subject. Amidst these stalwarts, India, with its rich traditional learning and tech-embrace, secures an admirable eighth spot. Its contributions are not just numerous, but contextually rich, reflecting its unique confluence of culture and technology.

Workplace Learning: The Office Archives

As we get to explore the academic journey of Workplace Learning, yet another pillar of research associated with the phenomenon of reskilling, we see an intriguing timeline. While the seeds of interest to explore this subject were sown in 1988, it was the cusp of the new millennium that truly brought a flurry of scholarly attention to the subject. As the winds of change swept the workplace dynamics, research burgeoned.

On the global stage, the UK emerges as the vanguard of Workplace Learning discourse, closely trailed by Australia's innovative contributions and the United States' deep dives. The European continent adds its own rich narratives, with countries like the Netherlands, Germany, Cana da, Sweden, Finland, Belgium, and Norway crafting distinct chapters in this unfolding story. And yet, amidst this global force, India's voice seems subdued, signalling a potential treasure trove of untapped insights waiting to be explored.

Skill Acquisition and Skill Development: The Chronicle of Mastery

The journey of Skill Acquisition and Development research started with tentative steps in the early years of the twentieth century. However, as the 1980s dawned, a clear shift was palpable. A significant surge in scholarly focus emerged, amplifying even further as the 2000s rolled in, indicating the world's realization of its utmost importance.

At the forefront of this academic expedition is the United States, wielding its scholarly might and significantly shaping the discourse. Further UK's methodical studies, Australia's applied research, Canada's comprehensive surveys, Germany's analytical endeavours, and the unique perspectives from South Africa, Japan, Spain, and the Netherlands enrich the mosaic. India steps in with confidence, clinching a commendable sixth position, contributing its own tales of talent and training to the global narrative.

Lifelong Learning: A Journey Without End

In the academic landscape, the theme of Lifelong Learning traces its origins to the 1950s. Yet, it was the 1990s that truly marked its watershed moment. Since then, this subject has been captivating researchers around the globe.

This is another area where researchers of The United States and the United Kingdom lead in charting its depths, followed closely by researchers from countries such as Australia, Germany, Spain, Canada, China, Italy, the Netherlands, and Greece. Amidst this global chorus, India's voice remains subdued, hinting at untapped potential and unexplored territories of knowledge on the subject in the country.

Insights from the Past; Pathways for the Future

The global research arena is resplendent with studies on Reskilling, Workplace Learning, and Lifelong Learning. While the scope for further exploration is vast, the existing literature in Self-Directed Learning, Skill Acquisition, and eLearning/mLearning offers a robust foundation for the global workforce reskilling imperative.

The turn of the millennium was characterized by profound revelations about the dimensions of Reskilling. Billet's (2000) discourse underscored the transformative impact of digitization on workplaces, necessitating an urgent recalibration of skills. Drawing correlations between organizational culture, technology, and reskilling, he threw light on the changing contours of the modern workplace.

In the same epoch, Darwin's work resonated with insights on the significance of culture and mentorship, while Reio delved into the intriguing realm of a learner's curiosity and information-seeking tendencies. Lombardo and Eichinger presented a conceptual masterstroke, laying down the paradigms of Change Agility, Mental

Agility, Results Agility, and People Agility, which Kenneth later empirically validated.

Amidst these multifaceted discussions, one consistent narrative emerged: the undeniable role of mindfulness in enhancing an individual's learning acumen. The collective wisdom from these studies established a crucial edict – in an era of relentless technological advancement, the clarion call is not just for sporadic upskilling but for continuous reskilling. Here, both the individual and the institution shoulder a collective responsibility, forging a path towards a resilient and adaptive future.

Unravelling Reskilling: Organizational Dynamics

In the early dawn of the new millennium, 2002 witnessed an academic fervour. Gary Fempleton, Bruce R. Lewis, and Charles pioneered a metric to gauge organizational learning. Their revelation was profound: true learning organizations kindle an intrinsic drive in employees, urging them to venture into the realms of self-driven skill acquisition.

Yet, what constitutes such a learning-centric environment? Their probe unearthed a myriad of factors. It is not merely about embracing technological shifts or fostering transparent dialogues. It hinges on robust performance evaluations, aligning individual aspirations with organizational milestones, and crafting experiential odysseys like job rotations. An organization that seamlessly weaves social learning, astute design, and adept management of knowledge capital fosters an ecosystem where learning is not just encouraged, it is inherent.

Meanwhile, contemporaries Michael Beer and Sumnatra Ghosal illuminated another dimension, heralding culture, and leadership as the guiding aspect for employees on their learning trajectories. This hypothesis was not a fleeting whisper; its resonance was later reaffirmed by Prabha Renuka & Hopro Frederick in 2014. These intellectual pursuits reached a singular conclusion: organizations that sculpt an ambiance of ceaseless self-enhancement do not just foster innovation; they usher in an era where value creation becomes a harmonious duet between the institution and its members.

Such was the magnetism of these theories that eminent scholars, including Michael Beer (2002), Muasaad Alrasheedi, & Luiz Fernando Capretz (2013), delved deep into articulating the pivotal role organizations play in reskilling.

As the clock ticked into 2003, Boud et al. introduced a refreshing refrain to this melody. They evoked the imagery of 'communities of practice,' emphasizing that true learning is not always a solitary quest. Sometimes, it is in the collective cadence of peers, in shared pursuits and mutual inspirations, that the most profound skills are honed.

The years 2005 to 2008 heralded a deeper foray into understanding reskilling. These periods saw the research spectrum oscillate from the allure of technology to the more personal, intrinsic facets of learners.

In 2005, Agnes Kukulska-Hulme and John Traxler, both erudite in their pursuit, dissected the intricate weave of factors determining self-driven learning. Their explorations ventured beyond the mere gadgets and pixels of technology. Yes, technology played its part, but what about the learner's sense of possession over their own learning journey? Or the societal currents influencing their zeal? The digital prowess of the learner, and not to forget, the instructor's adeptness in this techno-scape, emerged as pivotal. But technology was only one chapter of this narrative. The ways learning was assessed and how institutions scaffolded these endeavours were equally seminal.

With the dawn of 2006, Lohman's introspection shifted the lens back to the learners, with the spotlight on their inner terrains. What fuels an employee's thirst for knowledge? How does the availability of time, or the closeness they feel to their colleagues, influence this? The logistical dimension, encompassing resources for skilling, intertwined with the deeper psychology of self-belief, proactiveness, and a genuine ardour for learning.

By 2008, Berg et al. layered this discourse further. Beyond the tangible and the psychological, they ushered in the demographic dimension. Age, gender, the corridors of formal education treaded, range of professional experiences, and the tenure in current roles – each aspect was meticulously dissected. But alongside these external markers, they delved into the heart of personal traits – how agile is one in embracing new knowledge? How vast or narrow is the chasm between one's current skill set and the new? And, perhaps most poignantly, they explored the silent spectre of resistance to reskilling.

Berg's revelations resonated deeply, highlighting a symbiosis – the synergy between the individual's organic learning within their work environment and the overarching ethos of a learning-centric organization. This narrative, once scripted, found echoing validations in the scholarly pursuits that followed, cementing these insights into the broader reskilling canon.

The late 2000s and early 2010s brought an amplification in our understanding of reskilling, meshing the ambiance of the learning setting with the tools and strategies employed, all underlined by intrinsic personal characteristics.

Jacobs et al., in 2009, cast a discerning eye on the canvas of the learning environment. Where did learning unfold? How meticulously were these experiences crafted and curated? Beyond the content and the learner, they underscored the role of the custodian of this journey – the trainer or facilitator. Their lens highlighted the dynamism between structured and unstructured learning moments, elucidating the importance of both in the mosaic of workplace learning.

Taiwan, in the same year, introduced a playful twist. The world of games, with their engagement and immersive qualities, was not just for entertainment. They were potent tools, amplifying motivation and elevating the efficacy of learning endeavours.

Kyndt et al., Ellstrom, Billett, Darwin, Ortenblad, and Wallo, spanning from the turn of the century to the contemporary moment of 2022, threaded together a compelling narrative. The ambiance of an organization, it's very DNA, influenced how employees embarked and progressed on their reskilling quests. Elements like a feedback-rich environment, opportunities for coaching and being coached, the ebb and flow of information, and the tools facilitating communication and innovation were not mere accessories. They were the lifeblood. Central to this discourse was the design of the roles employees inhabited. Dynamic roles, characterized by rotations and variety, acted as catalysts, propelling employees into new learning arcs.

Robert Eichinger, in 2012, added depth to this canvas, sculpting a framework to understand and gauge learning agility. This was not just about raw intellect or the accumulation of knowledge. Eichinger's construct ushered together openness to new experiences, meticulousness in approach, astute interpersonal interactions, and the primal foundation of common sense. Each aspect highlighted the nuanced dimensions that shape an individual's agility in adapting, learning, and thriving in ever-evolving workscapes.

The period spanning 2013 to 2017 witnessed a pivotal turn in the reskilling discourse, synthesizing technology's transformative role with the deeply personal dimensions influencing learning adoption.

As 2013 dawned, researchers delved into the increasingly digital realms of learning. The technological tools were not just novel gadgets; their adoption was contingent upon how intuitive they were ('Perceived ease of use') and the tangible value they brought to the learning experience ('Perceived usefulness'). Beyond the tools, cultural contexts played a pivotal role, signifying that the medium and the environment were inseparable when fostering effective learning. The story continued to evolve with Hurlye and Jasen Haag later positing that the very adoption of mobile tech-based platforms could be viewed as a yardstick for organizational evolution. They echoed the broader narrative – learning in the digital age was not merely about content. It was an intricate dance between the platform, the content, and the learner.

Manuti's 2015 exploration refined the lens further. The magnifying glass was turned towards the role of one's academic background and professional experiences in shaping workplace learning. This was not about formal training sessions but the vibrant, informal moments of insight and growth. These unstructured, often serendipitous learning moments individualized the learning journey, equipping organizations to navigate the complex waters of workplace evolution.

Kenneth De Meuse, in 2017, undertook an intellectual expedition, sifting through a plethora of studies to craft a holistic construct. This was not just a measurement tool but a compass pointing towards the attributes defining one's agility and intrinsic motivation to learn. Preeti Nandwal & Dr. Anukul M. Hyde delved into the demographic undertones of this journey. Age, professional rank, academic qualifications – these were not mere statistics. They were potent influencers shaping how receptive and agile one was in their learning trajectory. Echoing the findings from the past fifteen years, they reinforced a recurring theme: reskilling was choreographed by a blend of personal attributes, the environment, and the tools facilitating the journey.

The threshold of 2019 marked a turning point in the discourse surrounding reskilling. The research conducted in this year seemed to suggest a growing complexity, an intricate weave of human psychology, organizational culture, technology adoption, and individual attributes.

Alexandra Levit's findings offered an intriguing dimension to the idea of learning agility. It is a notion that combines an openness to fresh information with the capability to harness and execute based on new insights. While this trait may seem innate for some, Levit proposed that it was not an exclusive domain. Through the nurturing of certain habits and management styles, an environment conducive to learning agility can be fostered. What's more, those with this trait are not confined to traditional paths, demonstrating that non-linear experiences can be valuable wellsprings of professional growth.

Rahmi Baki & Burak Bigoren's meta-analysis wove technology seamlessly into this narrative. Their synthesis of 203 studies elucidated that the ease with which one can engage with a technology (PEOU) and the tangible value that the technology provides (PU) stand as twin pillars driving the adoption of technology-based learning. They expanded this understanding by breaking down PEOU and PU into sub-factors like self-efficacy, enjoyment, anxiety, and subjective norms. Syed Abdul, Abdul Waheed, and Yuan's subsequent work in Taiwan reinforced this, linking PEOU and PU as pivotal determinants when embracing innovations such as mobile and Virtual Reality platforms for learning.

Simultaneously, the work of Noura A. Alsheikh threw light on another angle – leveraging Big Data and cutting-edge technologies to provide a more personalized, tailored learning experience. This bespoke approach recognizes that every learner is unique, and their learning paths should reflect this individuality.

Arten Chelovechkon & Benjamin Spain's research added further nuance by identifying communication technology and time self-management as critical elements influencing self-driven skill acquisition. It is evident that in the era of digital learning, it is not just about the technology. It is about how individuals interact with and manage these tools, merging self-discipline with technological capability.

The post-2019 landscape in the realm of reskilling research reveals an increasingly intricate interplay of factors, encompassing social, psychological, technological, and institutional aspects.

Government's Role and Demographic Considerations: The recognition of the role of the state in advancing education and fostering an inclusive environment for an ageing population, as posited by Narot et. al (2021), underscores the importance of policy and demographic considerations in reskilling debates.

Employee Behaviour and Attitudes: Kar et.al (2021) illuminated the complex relationship between employees' aspirations, their actual behaviour, and resistance to reskilling. The intervening role of experience and education further complicates this relationship, suggesting that reskilling is not a uniform process but varies based on personal attributes.

Psychological Aspects of Learning: The spotlight on factors like curiosity and openness by Yap et. al (2021) brings to the forefront the mental and emotional attributes that drive learning. This was taken a step further by Ali et. al (2022), emphasizing the significant role emotions play in the learning journey.

Technological Innovations and their Implications: Sanchez et. al's (2021) work on gamification underscores the potential of technological advancements to reshape the learning landscape by making it more engaging and interactive.

Outcomes and Impacts of Workplace Learning: The link between workplace learning and diverse outcomes like job satisfaction, turnover intentions, and career success, as suggested by Rowden (2002) and Lehtonen et. al (2022), provides invaluable insights for organizations.

This positions reskilling not just as a tool for individual growth but also as a mechanism that can influence organizational health and performance.

Holistic Frameworks: Tioiviainen et. al (2022) offers a comprehensive approach, outlining how global worker learning can translate to tangible organizational benefits, such as increased productivity. This macro perspective serves as a crucial reminder of the broader implications of reskilling initiatives.

Learning Agility and Organizational Culture: The emphasis on learning agility, especially in the works of Dixon (2022) and Liu et. al (2022), paints it as a critical variable in the reskilling equation. This agility, combined with the overarching organizational culture, significantly influences the trajectory of workplace learning.

Mental and Emotional Flexibility: Naicker et.al (2021) suggest that it isn't just about having the right skills or tools but possessing the mental and emotional dexterity to navigate the challenges and uncertainties that come with reskilling.

Demographic Variables and Perception: While demographics often play a part in many sociological and psychological studies, Ocak et.al (2022) challenge the conventional wisdom by positing that age, gender, experience, etc., might not be as significant as once thought, at least in the context of lifelong learning perceptions.

Flexible Career Attitudes: Moon et. al (2022) emphasizes the need for flexible career perspectives. As industries and jobs evolve, so too must the attitudes and perceptions workers hold about their roles and the future of work.

Role of Education in Holistic Development: The assertion that education is not just about skills but also enhancing quality of life, fostering active ageing, and promoting lifelong learning underscores the transformative power of education. It plays a critical role in not only reskilling but in shaping a holistic and fulfilling life journey.

Outcomes of Employee Learning: Strengthening professional identity as an outcome indicates that learning goes beyond acquiring new skills. It significantly shapes an individual's sense of self and position in the professional world.

Variety of Influential Factors: The diverse list of elements like technology, motivations (both intrinsic and extrinsic), instructor competence, social access, feedback mechanisms, self-regulation, and self-determined learning highlight the multifaceted nature of the reskilling process. It is not just about learning new things but the environment, motivations, tools, and methodologies that influence this learning.

Learning Methodologies: The emphasis on different learning methods, from communities of practice to self-regulated learning, suggests that there is no one-size-fits-all approach to reskilling. It is a dynamic process, influenced by individual preferences, organizational structures, and the nature of skills being acquired.

The trajectory of research on reskilling has evolved over time. Initially, the focus was largely on the inherent attitude and ability of individuals to learn new skills, coupled with the influence of organizational structures such as culture and value generation. As technology became increasingly embedded in workplaces, research began emphasizing the importance of leveraging technology in the reskilling process. More contemporary studies delve into the nuanced aspects of individual perceptions and the motivational components that drive self-directed learning in the context of reskilling.

Research delving into industry-specific reskilling narratives has gained traction over time. The healthcare industry, in particular, has been a focal point for many such studies, largely because healthcare professionals face real-time, high-stakes situations where the precision and efficacy of their skills can directly influence outcomes. Every interaction, every patient dealt with, is an experiential moment that can refine their proficiency. Besides healthcare, the educational sector, manufacturing, and construction industries have also been subjects of scrutiny in terms of reskilling experiences.

In earlier times, around 1981, Apple's work highlighted how industrial transformations were leading to a capitalist influx in the educational realm. This work pointed towards the pivotal role schools play in ideologically shaping the future workforce. Much of the initial research on reskilling was rooted in the education sector, exploring the retraining of educators to cope with evolving pedagogical needs and methodologies.

Sandholtz's research in 2002 took a deep dive into educators' experiences within reskilling programs, trying to discern what kinds of opportunities were most coveted by teachers within these initiatives. The conclusions drawn were illuminating. For reskilling endeavours in education to be successful, the learning environment for teachers needs to be broadened. Only by creating more diverse and expansive learning avenues can there be a higher probability of teachers willingly embracing those opportunities. However, the factors influencing a teacher's reskilling journey are multifaceted. It is not just about the individual's disposition. It also involves the practices and cultural environment of their specific department, the governance structures at the school level, and overarching national educational policies. These myriad dimensions synergistically shape how and what experienced educators opt to learn.

Research has delved deep into the unique challenges and experiences associated with the reskilling of educators. A notable study by Bakkenes et al. in 2010, which followed the journeys of 94 teachers across six year-long learning programs, categorically highlighted the diversity of these experiences. Teachers, during their reskilling processes, engaged in a spectrum of learning activities. These included experimental approaches, introspective analysis of personal practices, drawing inspiration from peers, confronting challenges, resisting reverting to old methodologies, and in some cases, even avoiding learning. Remarkably, these mostly self-directed activities correlated strongly with salient learning outcomes that teachers reported, which ranged from evolutions in their knowledge and beliefs to emotional shifts and practical transformations.

Yet, the success of these learning activities was not solely based on individual agency. The broader context in which these teachers operated played a pivotal role. A study analyzing the conversational patterns and work-centric discussions among educators discovered that specific contextual factors heavily influenced their learning and practices. This points towards the need for an ecosystem that promotes positive interactions and constructive discourse.

The idea of self-driven learning, or "heutagogy," emerged as a significant theme in some studies. Notably, the perception educators held regarding the implementation of this concept was found to be crucial. Their perspective on self-determined learning was a determinative factor in sculpting effective and enduring professional development programs.

Associations or collectives provided crucial support structures for educators, often acting as a bridge across isolated teaching environments. A case in point was a study in Rwanda that highlighted how an English language teachers' association fostered networking, knowledge dissemination, and skill enhancement among its members.

Recent times, marked by the advent of remote learning, presented a new set of challenges. Webb's 2021 study offered insights into teachers' firsthand experiences as they navigated the shift from traditional face-to-face instruction to a remote learning paradigm.

Additionally, a study from Malaysia outlined several pivotal components for the effective reskilling of educators. These encompassed course design intricacies, practical exercises, simulations, educators' preparedness levels, focused upskilling training, and even real-world industrial experiences.

The field of education undeniably underscores the paramount importance of reskilling, where the inclination towards self-direction and the practical application of new competencies stand out as pivotal. These elements are not merely confined to the realm of academia. A parallel can be drawn with the healthcare sector, another arena rife with reskilling endeavours, as discerned from myriad research studies.

One such groundbreaking revelation from 2002 by Atack et al. brought to the fore the efficacy of web-based pedagogy in nursing education. It was not just the digital medium that was instrumental. Several other determinants played a collective role in shaping the nurses' online learning journeys. These encompassed educators, peer interactions, technological underpinnings, course blueprint, and the overall ambiance of the learning milieu. The synergy of these factors determined the success trajectory of nurses engaging in web-based upskilling.

Delving further into healthcare reskilling, simulation-based methodologies emerged as a potent tool. The power of simulation lies in its dual capacity: it is not only an effective training modality but also serves as a controlled and secure environment. Irrespective of the participants' expertise gradient, simulations enabled them to handle emergencies that mirror real-life healthcare scenarios. The essence of these simulations is to seamlessly transition from theoretical knowledge to tangible application, ensuring that patient safety — an uncompromisable tenet of healthcare — remains the fulcrum.

However, not all learning avenues in healthcare follow structured reskilling pathways. A particularly illuminating set of semi-structured dialogues with internal medicine physicians painted a distinct picture. It surfaced that the acquisition of new knowledge and skills by these practitioners was intrinsically woven into their daily clinical engagements. Their learning curve was heavily influenced by immediate patient care challenges, as opposed to overarching objectives aimed at enhancing professional competencies. This stresses the importance of experiential learning in the medical realm, where every patient interaction can be a rich reservoir of knowledge and skill enhancement.

The realm of medical education offers a fascinating collection of continuous learning, much of which is steeped in practical experiences and direct patient interactions. As noted, advice, feedback, and subsequent performance of healthcare practitioners are often inextricably linked to real-time patient conditions. For many, the clinical conundrums presented by specific patient cases, alongside deliberations with peers about those cases, form the bedrock of professional growth. Traditional avenues of learning, such as structured teaching or dedicated upskilling sessions, while valued, often play a secondary role when juxtaposed against the treasure trove of learning that arises from direct clinical encounters.

It is telling that the journey of skill acquisition for medical professionals is often more serendipitous than systematic. Their proficiency evolves more from experiential engagement rather than consciously pursued formal education. This spontaneous, situation-driven learning forms the essence of situated learning in the realm of medical education.

Further enriching this educational landscape is the existence of dual communities within faculty development programs. One community germinates from within the cohort undergoing faculty development, fostering collaboration, shared experiences, and mutual growth. This community thrives on several pillars, including the participants themselves, the program's structure, its content, the facilitator's guidance, and the overarching context within which the program is delivered.

Simultaneously, another community bubbles in the real-world clinical or academic settings. This 'workplace community' is characterized by the interplay of relationships, established networks, organizational ethos, specific teaching tasks, and the availability of mentoring. These elements collectively sculpt the learning experiences of medical professionals.

For a faculty development model to be truly effective, it is imperative that it takes into account the intricacies of both these communities. A holistic approach ensures that both individual and collective learning trajectories are optimized.

In sum, a nuanced perspective of medical education, informed by the principles of situated learning, advocates for a teaching methodology that not only emphasizes active participation but also leverages community-driven processes. Such an approach ensures a harmonious melding of both individual and collective educational journeys, elevating the overall standard of medical education.

The healthcare sector, with its intrinsic complexity and ever-evolving challenges, demands an unwavering commitment to continuous learning and skill enhancement. As such, an emphasis on faculty development and student training becomes paramount, especially when rolling out assessment programs that further the cause of effective learning.

Indeed, modern advancements in educational technology, such as augmented reality (AR), herald a new dawn for medical education. AR, with its capability to immerse learners in hyper-realistic scenarios, promotes situated learning experiences. This, in turn, nurtures complex medical learning and aids in the effective transfer of skills. In essence, AR epitomizes the transformative potential of technology in shaping the future contours of medical education.

Reflecting on the reskilling narratives emerging from the healthcare domain, it is evident that there is a pronounced emphasis on skill proficiency and its real-time application on the job. The efficacy of continuing professional development hinges on several key factors. It requires technology-backed courses that are not just rooted in robust theoretical frameworks but are also interactive, easily accessible, and economically viable. Of course, this presumes that participants come equipped with both the necessary devices and a foundational level of tech-savviness.

Furthermore, the healthcare sector's multifaceted nature demands reskilling in areas like sober environments, mental health support systems, syringe distribution programs, and ensuring continuity in patient care. It's also worth noting the paramount importance of attributes like self-care abilities, motivational levels, an internal locus of control, and the availability of a robust social support mechanism, especially when facilitating transitions for individuals post confinement.

The global pandemic brought forth unprecedented challenges, emphasizing the need for nimble adaptations. Clinical areas underwent swift reconfigurations, departments deemed non-essential were temporarily shuttered, and there was a concerted effort towards reskilling and reorienting staff. This agility showcased the resilience and adaptability of healthcare professionals, particularly nurses and midwives.

At the heart of effective healthcare delivery is the core competency of clinical reasoning. For physicians, it's imperative to weave context seamlessly into the clinical process, ensuring that diagnoses and treatments are both precise and holistic. Moreover, the healthcare sector's dynamics underscore the confluence of physician competencies with leadership skills. It is a synergy that fosters lifelong learning and propels healthcare professionals towards excellence.

Ultimately, in the healthcare realm, the yardstick of success is not merely about acquiring competencies. Instead, it is about the tangible translation of these newly acquired skills into enhanced patient care. The ethos here is simple: action trumps intent, and performance reigns supreme.

The automotive sector, standing at the crossroads of rapid technological innovation and traditional modes of operation, has witnessed a paradigm shift with the onset of Industry 4.0. As noted from research in India, there's a conspicuous dearth in literature concerning the ramifications of Industry 4.0 on the workforce. Notably, most academic discourse has been skewed towards the intricacies of technology adoption, leaving workforce implications largely uncharted.

Zooming into South Africa's motor industry, an eye-opening study in 2021 unravelled the intricate dynamics at play within the automotive workforce. The findings, garnered from interviews with participants from three prominent motor companies, paint a rather unconventional picture. Contrary to expectations, autoworkers displayed a palpable inclination towards self-employment, driven by the looming spectre of job insecurity endemic to traditional industrial roles. In a bid to diversify their income streams and perhaps seek stability, many have ventured into realms like FOREX, Bitcoin mining, and even pondered career shifts towards fields like computer science and agriculture. Within this backdrop, the drive to upskill for future roles within the automotive sector seemed lukewarm, at best. The implications are clear: there's a compelling need for automotive sector workers to delve into skillsets that are immune to automation, encompassing both technical and non-technical job domains.

Oliva-res et al. (2022) chimed in on this dialogue, emphasizing the imperatives of recalibrating the education system to align with the prerequisites of smart manufacturing. The spectre of autonomous vehicles, set to revolutionize the transport sector, further complicates the landscape. These vehicles are perceived as potent disruptors, poised to render many traditional jobs obsolete. Hence, it's imperative for stakeholders to prioritize reskilling initiatives, alongside concerted efforts in public engagement and awareness campaigns, ensuring a seamless transition.

Past studies mapping out the contours of the automotive sector underscore two salient points: the glaring absence of comprehensive research on worker reskilling and a discernible trend of workers gravitating towards self-employment over reskilling or transitioning to new roles within the industry.

The construction and mining sectors are at a crossroads. As they grapple with the ripple effects of technological advancements like Construction 4.0 and mining automation, there's a pressing need to recalibrate the workforce, ensuring they're aligned with the ever-evolving job design and requirements.

Construction 4.0, the industry's response to the overarching influence of Industry 4.0, underscores a profound transformation in job design, urging professionals to acquaint themselves with the latest developments to ensure adaptability. Mining, on the other hand, is in the midst of an automation revolution. This transformation, brought to the fore by advancements in automation and robotics, coupled with the systemic challenges posed by the COVID-19 pandemic, is rapidly pivoting the industry towards minimizing human intervention in core operational processes.

Parades et al. (2021) offer a bird's eye view of the overarching challenges and potential solutions, laying out a roadmap for governments. They delve into policies aimed at offsetting the potential adverse impacts, underlining the imperatives of reskilling miners and implementing tax transfers. Modimogale et al., 2021, approach the challenge from a different vantage point, harnessing the dynamic capability theory. They scrutinize the skill transition process, especially within the context of the influx of innovative technologies, characterizing this new epoch.

Importantly, professional learning within these sectors isn't just about skill acquisition. It's a holistic approach that synergizes innovation, professional development, and individual growth. This learning is often fostered through reflective practices and interactions at the workplace, cementing the idea that upskilling is as much an organizational responsibility as it is of the professionals.

However, when juxtaposing the progress across sectors, a clear dichotomy emerges. While sectors like education and healthcare have been proactive, diving deep into the reskilling matrix and charting their path, others appear to be at a nascent stage. Their focus, for now, is predominantly on recognizing the evolving job designs and the consequent need for reskilling. But the depth, exploring the modalities and dynamics of reskilling, remains largely untapped.

Means of Reskilling

The multifaceted nature of reskilling necessitates a variety of approaches, each catering to specific needs and contexts. The methods recommended from past studies underscore the breadth and depth of potential interventions, from harnessing narratives to leveraging advanced technological platforms.

Narratives stand out as one of the earlier and more fundamental means. Their potency lies in their ability to convey complex, nuanced information, often tacit, in a digestible format. Narratives bridge the chasm between explicit and tacit knowledge, making the latter accessible without a need for it to be painstakingly articulated. As a storytelling mechanism, narratives allow learners to glean insights from lived experiences, providing context and depth.

Linde (2001) champions another interesting approach: archival systems. These systems, such as 'lessons learned' repositories or video-record databases, serve as reservoirs of tacit knowledge. They are designed to capture, store, and relay experiential knowledge, offering a tangible platform for learners to access and absorb this knowledge. The effectiveness of such systems, as Linde suggests, hinges on meticulous design, ensuring that they cater to the nuances of tacit knowledge transfer.

Another significant finding is the pedagogic potential of work itself. Everyday work activities, often overlooked as mundane tasks, emerge as potent learning grounds. A quantitative study underscored this aspect, revealing that individuals often learn more from their routine tasks than from explicit guidance from seasoned colleagues or supervisors. This underscores the value of experiential learning, where professionals learn 'on the job', navigating challenges, making decisions, and iterating their approaches in real-time.

Modern methods like massive open online platforms, personalized learning, and Education 4.0 indicate the increasing role of technology in reskilling. They offer scalability, flexibility, and customization, catering to a global audience with varied needs.

The means of reskilling are as diverse as the challenges they seek to address. Whether through the age-old art of storytelling or cutting-edge online platforms, the goal remains consistent: to equip professionals with the skills and knowledge they need to thrive in ever-evolving landscapes.

The emphasis on competency-based education as highlighted by both Garavan & McGuire in 2001 and Biemans et al. in 2004 showcases a paradigm shift towards more tangible, measurable outcomes in education. Competency-based education pivots around acquiring specific skills or competencies rather than the mere accumulation of knowledge. However, as pointed out, there is a critical need for consensus on defining these competencies. Without standard parameters, measurements can become inconsistent and unreliable.

This approach is not just about individual learning but extends to a broader ecosystem. The interconnectedness of various activity systems and organizations, each with its distinct tradition, domain of expertise, and language, hints at a more distributed and holistic approach to learning. This holistic perspective is underscored by the importance placed on the contributions of clients or users, emphasizing the collaborative nature of modern workplaces.

Illeris's observations provide insights into the challenges faced by low-skilled workers. Limited information, inadequate advice, financial constraints, and time pressures can hinder their learning engagement. Addressing these barriers is critical for fostering an inclusive learning environment.

The concept of co-configuration settings further reinforces the intertwined nature of modern work and learning environments. In these settings, learning is not a solitary activity but rather a collaborative endeavour, spanning across multiple partners, over long durations, and often discontinuous timelines. This style of work and learning mirrors the nature of many modern industries where products and services are increasingly complex and require the collaboration of diverse stakeholders.

Lastly, the emphasis on Activity Theory and its counterpart, the theory of expansive learning, offer a framework that bridges the divide between individual learning and broader organizational learning. These theories suggest that true organizational learning is not just about individual growth but about collective, inter-organizational evolution. Such a perspective is invaluable in our increasingly networked and collaborative global work environment.

The focus on competency-based education, inter-organizational collaboration, and understanding barriers to learning presents a holistic view of reskilling, taking into account not just the individual learner but also the broader ecosystems in which they operate.

The discourse around training, particularly in the context of its application (or the lack thereof) in real-world workplace settings, is indeed complex. Key takeaways from the points highlighted are:

Training vs. Transferability: Even the most rigorous and effective training programs can fall short when it comes to application in the actual workplace setting. This gap between knowledge and actionable skills—often referred to as the 'transfer gap'—has been a recurring challenge in training and development. It underscores the need for training programs to not just teach but ensure that those teachings can be seamlessly applied in real-world contexts.

Situated Learning: This theory posits that learning is inherently tied to the context in which it is undertaken. For instance, a mechanic learns more effectively on the job, amidst the tools, noises, and challenges of a real garage, rather than a sanitized classroom. This highlights the importance of context, practice, and immersion in effective learning and potentially addresses the aforementioned 'transfer gap.'

Rethinking Professional Development: Webster-Wright's 2009 study challenges the traditional paradigm of professional development. Instead of merely delivering content, the focus should be on facilitating genuine professional learning that seamlessly integrates with day-to-day work tasks and responsibilities. This requires a holistic approach that considers the daily challenges, motivations, and contexts that professionals operate within.

Socio-Material Approach: The interplay between the tangible (material) and the intangible (social, cultural, cognitive aspects) in learning is gaining traction in research. It suggests that learning is not just a cognitive process but also deeply influenced by the material world and its tools, technologies, and environments. This intertwining of the material and discursive (social interactions, language, culture) aspects of learning suggests that both human and non-human factors are crucial in the learning process. For instance, a surgeon learning a new procedure does not just need to understand the technique but also needs to master the specific tools and technologies used.

Modern research into professional learning is advocating for a more integrated, contextually relevant, and holistic approach. Traditional models of isolated training programs might not be sufficient. Instead, ongoing, immersive, and context-driven learning experiences that consider both human and non-human factors are more likely to result in meaningful professional development and tangible improvements in workplace performance.

As we stand at the crossroads of the Fourth Industrial Revolution, the terrain of the professional landscape undergoes seismic shifts. Now, more than ever, the need for adaptable, resilient, and forward-thinking strategies in reskilling becomes undeniable. Let us take a deep dive into the avenues open to us:

The Disparity in Opportunities: The educational fabric is not woven uniformly for everyone. Factors such as age, educational background, occupation, and the industry of operation cast varying shades on one's learning experiences. This underscores the importance of a bespoke approach in reskilling initiatives, tailored to cater to these unique demographic nuances.

Bridging Work and Wisdom: In today's digital epoch, tasks are not just processes; they are infused with purpose. As we navigate the electronic corridors of our professions, embedding a rich blend of hands-on tasks with conceptual clarity becomes paramount. It is not just about the 'how' but also the 'why'.

The MOOCs Revolution: Massive Open Online Courses are not just transforming learning; they are democratizing it. Offering a vast ocean of knowledge, MOOCs stand as lighthouses for both academic aspirants and those thirsty for upskilling or reskilling. Their vast expanse caters to a myriad of learners, from the academically inclined to those seeking professional refinement.

The Personal Touch in Learning: Personalized learning is not merely a strategy; it is an invitation for learners to take the reins of their educational journey. By tailoring learning experiences to individual needs, we not only foster a sense of ownership but also pave the way for more efficient and engaging learning experiences. In the labyrinth of information, personalized learning serves as both a compass and a guide.

Future-Proofing Education: The next wave of education is not confined to brick and mortar. It will be digital, blended, and aligned with the United Nation's ambitious sustainable development goals. As universities evolve, they will form symbiotic relationships with cities, anchoring themselves as bastions of knowledge in a disrupted world. The recent international conference on innovative technologies showcased a glimpse into this future, with over 61 pioneering papers illustrating the marriage of technology and education.

When we speak of reskilling in this age, It is not just about imbibing new skills but about fostering an environment of continuous, contextual, and personalized learning. The future beckons, and with these strategies, we're more than equipped to answer its call.

Discovery of Job Transition Paths

In the evolving modern professional realm, static career paths are giving way to a dynamic ebb and flow of job transitions. With the turn of the decade, researchers are igniting a new frontier: the automation of job transition paths. While we stand on the threshold of this nascent research sphere, two compelling narratives emerge.

The first paints a canvas of skill transferability. Here, the question is not about mere skill acquisition but its potency across diverse roles and industries. A. Y. Huang and his team plunged into the depths of the hospitality industry's skill taxonomy. Their findings were revelatory: while the skills' scores of hospitality workers trailed, the soft skills they possessed became invaluable currencies in industries like healthcare and information technology. It is a reminder of the universality of certain skills – communication, problem-solving, and critical thinking. Such "transferable skills," as Daud et al. have articulated, are not just assets but lifelines for professionals, aiding in their seamless transitions across varied industrial landscapes.

However, this journey is not devoid of challenges. As we tread this path, choosing the right skill to hone becomes paramount, especially in a world where the market's pulse is mercurial, and the value of a skill can metamorphose overnight.

In the modern job market, Kokkodis & Ipeirotis ventured into uncharted territory. Their study presented a groundbreaking framework, tailor-made to pinpoint in-demand skills by scrutinizing the ever-shifting landscape for contract workers. When this visionary model was applied to a vast sea of 1.73 million job applications within an online labour market, the results were nothing short of spectacular.

An astounding upswing was observed — a potential revenue surge of 6% for the marketplace, a 22% leap in contractors' earnings, and a 47% expansion in the diversity of fresh skill acquisitions.

Yet, as we steer through this evolving paradigm, we notice tectonic shifts in sectors like manufacturing. As it embraces the winds of disruptive technologies, a clear trend emerges: a diminishment of low-skilled activities juxtaposed against the rising tide of high-skilled endeavours. Pontes et al. took a magnifying glass to this phenomenon, particularly focusing on the trajectory of low-skilled roles in the manufacturing realm. With the dawn of artificial intelligence and automation technologies, we stand on the precipice of a revolution — the birth of automated job/skill recommender systems. Such innovations promise to be guiding lights, aiding individuals in charting their job transition courses and sculpting their reskilling blueprints.

Diving deeper into these studies, an intriguing pattern unfolds. The DNA of job design and its interwoven skills emerge as pivotal touchstones in the odyssey of reskilling. It is evident that soft skills — those of communication, critical thinking, empathy, and resilience — are not mere adornments but the very backbone of the modern professional. As these skills transcend boundaries, spanning across diverse jobs and industries, the longevity and relevance of hard skills in the face of emerging competencies become the key markers guiding job transitions and individual reskilling narratives.

Self-Skilling: Research Revelations

Embarking on the Journey of Self-Driven Mastery

The saga of self-directed learning can be traced back to its nascent roots in 1956. As the years rolled by, the academic corridors of Kent State University resonated with a unique experiment. Kaplan and his team, in 1978, introduced an avant-garde academic program, where volunteers stepped into the shoes of educators. The academic fabric they wove was unlike any other; it nurtured self-directed learning and cultivated a profound sense of community. The revelations from this initiative were enlightening educators, when nestled in a dynamic ecosystem of openness and continued evolution, impart knowledge more effectively.

Gestrelius, a year later in 1979, painted a compelling canvas that encapsulated the essence of lifelong learning. Here, creativity was not just an expression but a learning catalyst. Flexibility was not mere adaptability, but a pillar of self-growth. In this realm, self-realization and self-directed learning became synonymous, echoing the evolving ethos of education.

AL-NA'AMA's work in 1980 magnified the importance of student perspectives in shaping the course of educational endeavours, emphasizing a deeper alignment with self-directed learning. But perhaps, Grow's 1990 study stands as a sentinel in this landscape. Grow sheds light on the evolving journey of learners through the stages of self-direction. Here, educators were not mere guides but were pivotal in either advancing or impeding this journey. Grow identified the pedagogical pitfalls as incongruities between the teaching style and the stage of the learner, a dance where the synchronicity of steps mattered.

A study delving into the role of experts painted a vivid picture: when students were shepherded by subject matter maestros, they not only devoted more time to self-driven studies but also outshone their peers. The prowess of tutors in imparting content knowledge and honing their tutoring skills became the lynchpin in bolstering self-directed learning.

In the realm of medical education, the recipe for effective learning was dissected further. It was a medley of sustained patient care, interactions with the faculty, a blend of collaboration and self-learning, faculty development, and a meticulous approach to assessment and feedback. Yet, amidst this, a revelation emerged: students might not always discern between a teacher's reservoir of knowledge and their knack for nurturing self-directed learning.

Medical professionals, in their continuing education endeavours, identify a series of stages within the self-directed learning journey. Beginning with the initial scrutiny of issues, they determine the worth of diving into a learning quest, following which they immerse themselves in acquiring newfound knowledge and honing their skills. The culmination of this odyssey is the tangible experience gleaned from what is been absorbed. However, a reflective pause post-practice could serve as a potent catalyst in transforming beliefs and perspectives.

For the realm of nursing, the Self-directed learning readiness scale was reimagined, gauging students' predispositions, competencies, and the inherent personality traits vital for SDL. A process-oriented teaching methodology, emphasizing SDL and Lifelong Learning (LLL), demands a comprehensive theoretical foundation, fortifying the conceptual base for educators.

In the digital age, tools like Scratch, designed for programming, emphasize 'tinkering' and collaboration, embodying the essence of fostering SDL. Guthrie's (2004) insights accentuate the nexus between 'engaged reading time' and SDL. Meanwhile, for medical apprentices, any dip in hands-on clinical practice or support can stunt the growth of SDL.

Self-assessment, steeped in awareness, becomes a cornerstone of SDL. The vast expanse of open online networks necessitates learner autonomy, an omnipresent engagement, and critical literacy. Mann (2011) underscores a spectrum of facets intertwining with SDL, from content and assessment to professional identity, spirited engagement, and the nuances of social learning. Ten et al. (2011) offer a panoramic view, linking SDL with self-determination theory, probing the interplay of assessments and faculty competence.

Exploring the intricate web of SDL, Brydges et al. (2012) offer a socio-contextual lens, emphasizing the criticality of self-management and regulation. Subsequently, Bok et al. (2013) delve into the synergy of assessment, feedback, and the dynamic of social interactions, spotlighting the mentor's role in the SDL.

Recent strides in research have pivoted around the myriad factors influencing self-directed learning (SDL). Young et al. (2014) distilled the essence down to reflection, cognition, and job design. Meanwhile, a trifecta of motivation, technology, and the role of assessments was meticulously examined by Boticki et al. in 2015. Wainer's study in the same year zeroed in on technology's pivotal role in SDL.

Subsequent studies unfurled facets like the interplay of technology with social media, its connection with student readiness, and its influence on mental agility. The emotional spectra of fun and fear associated with learning found a place too. Other avenues delved into include technology's synergy with problem-based learning (PBL), the balance between intention and its actual use, self-regulation in digital domains, the allure of mobile tech, and the intricate dance of perception and collaboration.

Cultivating Capacities for Self-Skilling

As the need for self-skilling gains traction, the pedagogic tools and techniques employed become paramount. Research paints a vibrant mosaic of methods to hone SDL abilities. Problem-Based Learning (PBL) emerges as a cornerstone, fostering a sense of inquiry and analysis. Competency assessments serve as milestones, gauging proficiency and skill levels.

Diverse strategies like conferencing, experiential learning, and interdisciplinary ventures offer rich, multifaceted learning experiences. Studies further advocate for individual development programs, robust educational assessments, and case-based learning to nurture SDL. Instruments such as SDL readiness scales provide valuable insights into a learner's predisposition for autonomous learning.

Innovative pedagogies like flipped classrooms turn traditional teaching on its head, empowering students to lead their learning journey. Additionally, harnessing socio-material processes offers a nuanced approach, integrating both the tangible and intangible facets of learning.

As we hurtle towards an increasingly digital future, understanding and enhancing SDL becomes an imperative, setting the stage for lifelong learners equipped for the challenges of tomorrow.

In a compelling 1992 study, Norman et al. delved deep into the impact of problem-based learning (PBL) on self-directed learning abilities. Their findings offer both revelations and reflections on PBL's efficacy. Contrary to initial assumptions, while PBL might not enhance content-free problem-solving skills, its long-term benefits on knowledge retention were noteworthy. Students not only showed improved retention over extended periods but also exhibited an enhanced capability to transfer conceptual knowledge to novel problems. Such findings underscore PBL's potential in facilitating the integration of basic science concepts into practical, clinical scenarios.

What's more, PBL curricula seem to have a magnetic pull, enhancing students' intrinsic interest in their studies. A notable byproduct? The nurturing of formidable self-directed learning skills. When pitted against lecture-based learning methods, PBL emerged as a clear front-runner. Students immersed in the PBL approach were not just motivated learners but also showcased superior abilities in problem-solving and knowledge recall.

Boyatzis' 1994 study added another dimension, highlighting the potential of a managerial assessment and development course. With its focus on a myriad of abilities, knowledge zones, and value themes, it served as another testament to the multifaceted ways SDL abilities can be honed.

Building on this, Gallagher's 1997 advocacy for PBL carried a ringing endorsement for its advantages, particularly in terms of long-term retention, conceptual understanding, and, of course, self-directed learning. Significantly, Gallagher did not just see PBL's relevance confined to higher education. He envisaged its seamless integration into younger classrooms, right from elementary to high school.

The narrative that emerges is clear: PBL is not just a pedagogical tool; it is a potent catalyst for nurturing curious, autonomous learners, ready to tackle the challenges of an ever-evolving world.

Levett's discerning 2005 analysis sheds light on the nuanced dynamics of self-directed learning (SDL) as an educational concept. While SDL was heralded for its transformative potential, the actualization often left much to be desired. A glaring gap emerged: a cohort of teachers and students ill-equipped to harness SDL's true potential. Yet, it is undeniable that when SDL is effectively integrated, it produces professionals with a distinct edge.

Diving into the intricacies of PBL (Problem-Based Learning), a study illuminates its profound impact on graduates. They didn't merely emerge with an enhanced academic grasp; their soft skills flourished. Armed with superior interpersonal skills, prowess in problem-solving, and a knack for information gathering, these graduates also showcased stellar task-supporting skills. The ability to plan, chart their course, and operate autonomously set them apart. Essentially, PBL isn't just about fostering cognitive and interpersonal strengths. It is a catalyst, refining graduates for success in the multifaceted realm of professional practice.

Mason's 2006 exploration brings to the fore a rather novel approach: conferencing. Presented as an avenue to nurture SDL capabilities, conferencing emerges as more than just a gathering. It's a potent tool, fostering learner autonomy, encouraging dialogue, and instilling self-directedness.

Jiusto's 2006 investigation into the Global Studies Program, a unique experiential interdisciplinary initiative, offers another dimension. Melding three distinct methods – IDEA (Individual Development and Educational Assessment), an internal project quality assessment protocol, and the SDLRS (Self-directed learning readiness scale) – the program promises a holistic approach to nurturing SDL. Jiusto's findings? An experiential learning environment isn't just about absorbing knowledge; it is a crucible where SDL and Lifelong Learning (LLL) abilities are honed to perfection.

An intriguing juxtaposition arises when one delves into the realms of case-based learning (CBL) and problem-based learning (PBL) in the medical education circuit of the United States. While both approaches aim to sculpt adept medical practitioners, a distinct inclination surfaces. Both faculty and students display a pronounced penchant for CBL over its PBL counterpart. The preference, however, doesn't necessarily adjudicate the superiority of one over the other. What it does spotlight is the urgency for a clearer conceptual framework around SDL, thereby optimizing the potential of PBL.

Diving deeper into the intricacies of self-directed learning, a compelling observation emerges. SDL is not a standalone entity but rather, it integrates seamlessly with Self-Regulated Learning (SRL). This symbiosis adds another dimension to the student's academic journey, empowering them not just in the acquisition of knowledge, but also in the selection and evaluation of learning resources.

Taylor and colleagues, in 2008, offer a sobering perspective. Despite the allure of both PBL and SDL, their full-fledged realization as educational concepts has been somewhat elusive for decades. The journey, though promising, has been riddled with challenges and unanswered questions.

Hung's explorations in 2010 and 2011 further underscore these complexities. With the advent of the Online Learning Readiness Scale (OLRS), there is evidence that senior students outpace their junior peers in SDL, self-efficacy, learning motivation, and learner control. Yet, as we inch towards integrating technology with PBL through blended problem-based learning (bPBL), a myriad of outcomes surface. While it undoubtedly elevates student motivation and collaboration, there is an undeniable undercurrent of concerns, especially cultural ones. As the world gravitates towards globalization, the educational realm must acknowledge that it does not promise uniform processes. The quest is to craft culturally sensitive alternatives that resonate universally.

A shift is palpable in the academic atmosphere. The landscape of learning, particularly in the United States, is undergoing a metamorphosis, embracing the allure of video-centric educational modules. As learners immerse themselves in this digital environment, a fascinating pattern emerges. Those naturally inclined towards proactive information-seeking and adept at managing their surroundings exhibit a heightened tendency to indulge in interactive note-taking, a pivotal tool that augments retention and comprehension.

Meanwhile, halfway across the globe in Taiwan, the educational realm is flirting with the 'flipped classroom' paradigm. By reversing the traditional learning structure, this model places emphasis on independent study through digital channels outside the classroom and more interactive, collaborative work during class. What is intriguing is the undeniable link between students' readiness for eLearning and their ensuing satisfaction and motivation levels within this flipped framework.

Yet, as we explore the myriad ways to foster self-directed learning (SDL), one crucial insight stands out. The inception of SDL aptitude does not begin in the corridors of higher education. Rather, it is the early embrace of a socio-material approach during initial school years that holds the key. By intertwining technology with education at a nascent stage, we sow the seeds for robust SDL proficiencies in the future.

Taking a closer look at the field of Engineering, the potential of a Problem-Based Learning (PBL) curriculum is evident. Not only does it sharpen the analytical prowess of the students, but it also instils metacognition—a heightened awareness of one's own thought processes, which is a cornerstone of SDL.

At its core, the journey of self-directed learning is deeply intertwined with individual attitudes and behaviours. These are not innate but moulded over time, with early educational experiences playing a cardinal role. Indeed, pedagogical methodologies wield immense power. They do not just transfer knowledge; they shape the very attitudes and behaviours conducive to nurturing the blossoming of self-directed learners.

Harnessing Self-Directed Learning to Amplify Self-Skilling Outcomes

The realm of Self-Directed Learning (SDL) is intriguing, not merely for the process it unfolds but for the tangible outcomes it brings forth. Over the decades, countless studies have endeavoured to demystify the inherent connection between SDL and the resultant self-skilling consequences.

Journeying back to 1975, the landscape of medical education served as a canvas for an experimental study, revealing insights that still resonate today. Contrary to a general belief that curating a uniform learning experience would yield similar outcomes for a cohort, the study unveiled a stark variance between group and individual learning. This underscored an immutable truth—the individual's role in their learning trajectory remains paramount, regardless of the external environment crafted for them.

This individual-centric approach to learning is further emphasized through the lens of self-motivation. As posited by certain studies, the mere act of setting proximal goals—a series of short-term targets leading to an overarching objective—serves as a catalyst. It does not just propel learners towards their goals but also kindles intrinsic interest, self-efficacy, and an array of competencies, thereby accentuating the self-skilling outcome.

In the dawn of the new millennium, Guthrie and his contemporaries revealed another facet of SDL. By meticulously interweaving SDL principles into the very fabric of instructional experiences, they showcased how such an approach can markedly enhance learning outcomes. One such domain that reaped the benefits was language acquisition via technology. By introducing pedagogic constructs that championed SDL, the entire experience of technology-aided language learning underwent a transformation.

Yet, as we navigate the vast ocean of eLearning, an underlying assumption often lurks beneath the surface. It presumes that learners innately possess a robust SDL capacity, enabling them to seamlessly assimilate the array of content presented. Such an assumption necessitates a recalibration of our instructional strategies. For the true potential of technology-based learning to be unlocked, a confluence is essential—a harmonious blend of technology's capabilities, astutely crafted instructional strategies, and the intricate psychological processes that underpin learning.

When it comes to self-skilling, SDL goes beyond being a mere component – it is the foundation upon which learning outcomes take shape. Extensive research consistently demonstrates the immense value and beauty that the right interventions bring to this process.

Self-Directed Learning (SDL) is not just a pedagogical approach or a trendy educational catchphrase. In essence, it is an empowerment tool, a foundational block for a resilient, adaptive, and independent future. As the world becomes increasingly volatile, the certainties of today may not remain the same tomorrow. It is in this shifting landscape that the merits of SDL truly shine.

Facing Economic Challenges: The modern era, with its rapid technological advancements, has brought with it the spectres of unemployment and underemployment. However, with SDL, individuals are better equipped to re-skill and up-skill, ensuring that they remain relevant and employable.

Mitigating Social Challenges: In a world growing increasingly digital, the chances of social isolation rise. SDL fosters a sense of curiosity and a desire for connection, driving individuals to seek out communities of interest and purpose, thereby reducing feelings of loneliness.

Becoming Self-reliant: At the heart of SDL lies the core principle of autonomous action. This isn't limited to just educational pursuits but extends to life skills, allowing individuals to lead independent, self-sufficient lives.

Extending the Benefits Beyond the Classroom: Organizations can tap into the principles of SDL to empower their customers. By facilitating customers to integrate resources, both their own and those provided by the business, there's a co-creation of value. This not only boosts customer satisfaction but also fosters loyalty.

Cognitive and Computational Benefits: From a cognitive standpoint, SDL allows learners to channel their efforts more productively. It also enhances retention and comprehension. On the computational side, the concept mirrors the realm of machine learning, where algorithms actively choose their data sets, optimizing the learning process.

Determinants of Successful SDL: The way individuals navigate their SDL journey greatly influences outcomes. Factors like motivation, internal locus of control, and self-efficacy, as highlighted by Boyer et al.'s meta-analysis, play pivotal roles in ensuring SDL's success.

A Lifelong Affair: SDL is not restricted to formal educational years. It is a lifelong commitment, a continuous journey of discovery and growth. Whether it is the challenges of online education or adapting to a new vocational role, SDL remains a trusted ally.

SDL is not just an approach—it is a mindset, a commitment to oneself. In an ever-evolving world, it offers the promise of adaptability, resilience, and growth. Institutions, businesses, and individuals who embrace SDL are not only preparing for the challenges of tomorrow but are also ensuring they thrive amidst them.

Role of SDL in Adult Learning and Technology Based Learning

Self-Directed Learning (SDL) holds paramount significance in the context of adult learning and technology-based instruction. As adults navigate the complexities of life and work, they often gravitate towards learning methodologies that respect their autonomy, cater to their unique learning needs, and allow them to integrate their real-world experiences.

Concept-oriented learning, which emphasizes concrete learning goals, hands-on real-world interaction, competence support through strategy instruction, autonomy via self-direction, and the camaraderie of collaboration, sits at the heart of adult learning theories. It seeks to bridge the gap between theoretical knowledge and its practical application, making learning both engaging and meaningful for adults.

One of the intriguing facets of adult learning is the idea of perspective transformation. Rooted in the intertwining elements of reification and reflectivity, perspective transformation represents the paradigm shifts that adults undergo as they re-examine and reinterpret their experiences, values, and beliefs. This transformative journey, inherently self-directed, underscores the importance of SDL in enabling adults to challenge and redefine their understanding of the world.

Adults, by virtue of their diverse experiences, often bring with them a myriad of learning needs, goals, and preferred modes of education. Unlike their younger counterparts, they have a clearer sense of purpose, are more self-aware, and often seek educational experiences that align with their aspirations. To this end, self-directed modular curriculums have proven to be immensely successful for adult learners.

These curriculums, whether delivered in a place-based setting or in distance formats, allow adults to tailor their learning experiences to their specific needs. While this modular and customized approach resonates deeply with adults, it may not necessarily hold the same appeal for younger learners, who might still be exploring their learning styles and objectives.

The rise of technology has further amplified the potential of SDL in adult learning. Online platforms inherently empower learners with a degree of control, letting them decide the pace, mode, and direction of their learning. However, it is crucial to understand that the level of self-direction and autonomy required might vary across different learning contexts. Even in an online environment, there might be situations where learners benefit from a guided approach, especially when it concerns complex topics. The challenge, then, is to harness technology not just as a medium of delivery, but as an enabler of personalized learning. Through thoughtful instructional design, technology can be leveraged to adapt and respond to individual student needs, ensuring that the learning experience is both enriching and effective.

The onset of the digital age, coupled with unexpected global events like the COVID-19 pandemic, has catalysed the need for adaptable and technologically adept learning platforms. eLearning emerged not only as a necessity but as an opportunity to reimagine the nature and methodology of education. The critical challenge, however, lies in designing interfaces that don't merely replicate traditional classroom settings but empower students to access a diverse array of resources and cultivate a culture of independent learning.

The COVID-19 pandemic has been an inflection point in examining the dynamics of eLearning. Various studies have delved into the factors that have influenced students' adoption of online education during this period. Among the significant predictors are entrepreneurial storytelling and the student mindset. The way educators communicate and resonate with their audience, and the predispositions and adaptability of students, play a substantial role in shaping the eLearning experience.

Moreover, the footprint of eLearning is not restricted to formal education sectors. The corporate world, driven by the imperatives of sustainability and green initiatives, is recognizing the value of "green digital learning." Such learning mechanisms serve a dual purpose: they are environment-friendly and champion the cause of sustainable solutions within industries. For instance, the banking sector's foray into eLearning demonstrates how effective online training can positively influence customer behaviour, such as the adoption of online banking practices.

Yet, the success of online education is not just determined by the content or the technology. The learners' self-regulated learning skills, their confidence in the digital realm (internet self-efficacy), and the quality of their interactions – both with the content and with their peers – are pivotal. Furthermore, personal demographic factors, such as age, gender, and educational background, also significantly influence learners' satisfaction levels and engagement with online platforms.

An intriguing observation has been the role of a student's intrapreneurial capabilities in the success of online learning. Those who demonstrate innovation within their organizational contexts, and possess a certain drive and initiative, often fare better in eLearning settings. This underscores the importance of fostering an entrepreneurial spirit, even in educational environments.

The ascent of technology-based learning is not just a response to changing global dynamics; it is an evolution that recognizes the intrinsic value of self-directed learning. This approach is especially pertinent for adults, who often seek to reskill or upskill in the face of rapidly changing professional landscapes. The emphasis on SDL in technology-based education ensures that learning remains a lifelong, adaptive, and empowering journey.

Principles of Self-Directed Learning for Skill Development

Self-directed learning (SDL) is rooted in the understanding that learners have innate capabilities and inclinations, and when given the right environment, can drive their own learning processes. Several principles underline this approach, and these have evolved over the years with research and experimentation in pedagogy. These principles are essential not only in the traditional educational context but also in the evolving landscape of self-skilling, which emphasizes adaptability, lifelong learning, and preparation for rapid professional changes.

The first characteristic of SDL is the acknowledgment that both the learner and the institution bring their unique perspectives on what is deemed essential. While an institution might emphasize specific knowledge areas, the learner might prioritize certain skills or knowledge based on their intrinsic motivation or professional aspirations. Bridging this gap and finding a middle ground is vital for successful SDL.

Central to the success of SDL is its alignment with the learner's individual needs and motives. This principle recognizes that learners come with a spectrum of experiences, aspirations, and capabilities. Rather than imposing a one-size-fits-all model, SDL encourages education systems to tap into these unique learner profiles. By doing so, it fosters confidence and bolsters the learner's ability to undertake independent learning endeavours.

However, one of the challenges in SDL is the potential internal resistances that learners might have, which could be due to previous educational experiences, preconceived notions about learning, or even fear of the unknown. Overcoming these barriers is pivotal for achieving the desired learning outcomes. Effective education design, thus, involves recognizing and addressing these internal forces, providing the necessary support, and gently nudging the learner towards the established goals.

Harrison's principles of SDL design provide valuable insights into how SDL can be effectively implemented:

Conceptual Framework: Having a clear theoretical or conceptual foundation helps learners understand the larger context of their learning journey. This gives them a map or a scaffold upon which they can build their knowledge.

Valued Alternatives: Recognizing that learning is not a linear path and offering various learning routes or methods ensures that learners can choose a path most aligned with their preferences, strengths, and goals.

Structured Support: While SDL emphasizes independence, it acknowledges that learners might need support, especially in the initial stages. By providing this support, educators ensure that learners are not overwhelmed and can eventually transition to more independent learning stages.

Maximum Feasible Choice: This is perhaps the cornerstone of SDL. Giving learners the autonomy to make decisions, be it in terms of the content, method, pace, or even assessment, ensures that they are invested in the learning process.

Self-directed learning (SDL) as a concept has been rooted in a variety of theoretical perspectives that seek to explain human behaviour and learning processes. The six theoretical positions highlighted—modelling, reinforcement, curiosity motivation, competency motivation, attribution theory and personal causation, and humanistic—each provide a lens through which the essence of SDL can be understood.

Modelling: Rooted in social learning theory, this emphasizes the importance of observation and imitation. Individuals learn by observing the behaviours of others and the outcomes of those behaviours. In the context of SDL, this implies that learners can become self-directed by observing and emulating self-directed behaviours in others.

Reinforcement: This theory posits that behaviours are shaped by their consequences. Positive reinforcements, like rewards or praise, can encourage self-directed behaviours, while negative reinforcements or punishments can discourage undesirable behaviours.

Curiosity Motivation: This is grounded in the intrinsic desire to know more. It suggests that individuals have a natural inclination to explore, discover, and understand, which can drive self-directed learning.

Competency Motivation: Here, individuals are motivated by the need to be competent and effective in their interactions with the environment. This positions SDL as a mechanism for individuals to achieve mastery and competence in their chosen fields.

Attribution Theory and Personal Causation: This theory looks at how individuals attribute causes to their successes and failures. Those who believe they have control over their learning outcomes are more likely to engage in self-directed learning.

Humanistic: Rooted in humanistic psychology, this theory emphasizes personal growth, autonomy, and self-actualization. It suggests that individuals are naturally inclined to grow and develop, and SDL aligns with this intrinsic drive.

Drawing from these theoretical positions, several educational practices emerged. Experiential learning emphasizes learning through experience and reflection; discovery learning focuses on learners finding out things for themselves; the open classroom approach prioritizes flexibility and learner autonomy; and structured individualization ensures that learners have personalized pathways to achieve their learning goals.

Furthermore, the importance of SDL becomes pronounced in diverse learning scenarios. Whether it is learners who cannot attend regular classes, diverse learning needs within a classroom, or prepping learners for independent learning, SDL provides a framework that is adaptable and effective.

Characteristics of a self-directed learner encompass both traditional aspects like discipline, focus, and commitment, and radical ones such as adaptability, questioning norms, and being open to new experiences. The recurring theme in their journey is the search for purpose and a driving force that propels them to learn.

These foundational studies and principles have indeed provided the scaffolding for modern interpretations of SDL, emphasizing its critical role in today's ever-evolving learning landscape. As self-skilling becomes increasingly important in our rapidly changing world, the principles of SDL offer insights and guidelines for effective lifelong learning.

The advent of Industry 4.0 has dramatically transformed the professional landscape, instigating an urgency to adapt or face the stark reality of redundancy. Businesses, employees, and even society at large are grappling with newly defined job expectations, prompting a monumental shift in skills and roles. This metamorphosis is not limited to a particular sector; its ripples are felt across industries, prompting a need for revolutionary reskilling.

Smart manufacturing, emblematic of Industry 4.0, is reshaping operational dynamics and job designs. There is a heightened focus on broadening knowledge and honing meta-skills, both becoming indispensable for treading through the complexities of the 21st century. As technology amplifies its influence, the human role in factories is undergoing a shift. The intricate dance between individuals and intelligent machines has taken centre stage, necessitating a recalibration of skills.

However, this seismic shift is not just confined to the factory floors or corporate boardrooms. Educational institutions, the bedrock of knowledge dissemination, are facing the heat. With the fourth industrial revolution upon us, educators are confronted with a dual challenge. Not only do they need to grasp these emerging technologies, but they must also embed them within their curriculum, ensuring that students are equipped for the future. The onus is not just on institutional reform; educators themselves must engage in active self-skilling. Only by immersing themselves in real-time experiences and simulations can they truly impart relevant knowledge. In essence, for teachers to shape the future, they must be adept at shaping their own.

Talent development, in today's rapidly evolving technological landscape, stands at a critical juncture. The stakes are high; existing employees grapple with the demands of a swiftly transitioning digital economy, while the upcoming generation—tomorrow's workforce—requires an education tailored to anticipated future roles and skill sets.

Historically, technological progression catalysed economic expansion, a cycle wherein certain jobs became obsolete while others sprouted anew. However, Industry 4.0, marked by exponential growth in technologies such as mobile internet, the internet of things, big data analytics, and artificial intelligence, deviates from this norm. While it promises unparalleled economic growth, it simultaneously casts a shadow of potential joblessness and unprecedented unemployment rates.

Yet, within this conundrum lies an immense opportunity. Reskilling can become the bridge that helps displaced workers transition to new, meaningful, and sustainable roles. But this shift does not just affect employment; it profoundly impacts an individual's professional identity.

A person's professional identity is closely interwoven with their role or occupation. Think of the labels we casually apply: taxi driver, professor, businessperson. These are not just designations but encapsulate a set of associated actions, behaviours, skills, and functions. The term "identity" transcends mere labels. It could denote a social category, distinguished by membership rules and characteristic behaviours.

Alternatively, it could spotlight a distinguishing trait, one that an individual holds with pride or sees as immutable, yet socially significant.

In the tumultuous landscape of Industry 4.0, these identities face inevitable transformation, raising poignant questions about individual and societal adaptability in an age of rapid change.

The journey of acquiring new skills is more than just the assimilation of knowledge; it is intrinsically tied to one's professional identity. As employees hone new skills and capabilities, they begin to align with different professional groups, potentially altering their perception of where they belong in the professional realm. This shift in identity is profound and can ripple through an individual's sense of self-worth, purpose, and career trajectory.

From an organizational perspective, there is a silver lining. Companies that champion and invest in comprehensive learning environments often reap dividends in innovation. The logic is straightforward: the broader the organization's scale of activities, the more diversified the learning experiences, and the more evenly the associated costs can be distributed. This wide-scale learning not only elevates individual competencies but, in the aggregate, propels the entire organization towards a more innovative and value-centric trajectory.

Central to this transformative journey is the role of the individual, acting as an agent of change. Their drive, curiosity, and commitment play a pivotal role in this metamorphosis of the workforce. Thus, diving deep into the intricacies of how individuals learn, adapt, and evolve becomes paramount. It is not merely about skilling up; it is about understanding the psyche of the modern learner, acknowledging their aspirations, and facilitating a pathway for them to redefine their professional identities in a dynamic world.

CHAPTER – 4

Key Concepts and Theories Related to Reskilling

Skills serve as the backbone of individual capability and collective economic vitality. But a skill is not just a static representation of what one knows; it is a dynamic capacity to perform, often in complex and changing situations. What makes a skill invaluable is not merely the underlying competence but its application in real-world contexts. Skills are not born; they are painstakingly learned, cultivated, and honed over time.

Skills are not monolithic entities but are made up of various defining attributes, as articulated by Cornford in 1996:

- Skill is learned, not innate.
- Skills are driven by motivation, purpose, and goals.
- Schemas serve as the intellectual building blocks for skilled performance.
- Both content and contextual knowledge are crucial for skill acquisition.
- Skills are brought to life in the presence of specific stimuli.
- Skilled performance requires problem-solving aptitude relevant to the context.
- Skill levels differ among individuals, pointing to the relativity of judgment.
- Standards of excellence set the benchmark for skilled performance.
- Skills are demonstrated through replicable actions.
- Mastery of skill demands a significant investment of time.

Not all skills are created equal or can be acquired in the same manner. Some skills are industry-specific, demanding specialized training programs, while others are more universal, gained through experience and ongoing engagement with work. Take, for example, a software engineer. The engineer needs not just to know how to code but to understand how to work within the contours of a team, how to navigate project management complexities, and how to problem-solve on the fly. In contrast, an artist needs a deep-rooted understanding of colour theory, materials, and techniques but also must understand market trends and audience engagement. These job-specific skills are the flesh and bones that build upon the skeletal framework of our more universal, foundational skills.

Furthermore, possessing a skill is only half the equation. The other half lies in the effective deployment of that skill in productive work settings. In essence, skills must be matched with opportunities where they can be put to optimal use for both individual growth and collective advancement. Skills should not exist in a vacuum; they require a conducive environment to grow and be meaningful. This necessitates a well-calibrated educational and workforce development system that can produce individuals who are not just skilled but are ready to apply those skills innovatively.

The interplay of upskilling and reskilling is an ongoing, fluid journey best understood through the lens of theories like the Theory of Work Adjustment (TWA) and Donald Super's concept of vocational maturity. According to TWA, individuals and their work environments are in a state of perpetual negotiation, striving to meet each other's needs and requirements. This ongoing adjustment makes the acquisition of new skills a necessity, not a choice.

Super's Career Model provides a structured framework for understanding this process, as represented in Figure 4.1. According to

Super, individuals go through various life stages—Growth, Exploration, Establishment, Maintenance, and Decline—each requiring different forms of skill acquisition and adaptation. This non-linear progression challenges the conventional wisdom that associates certain career behaviours strictly with chronological age. As individuals navigate these stages, their "self-concept," or understanding of their own capabilities and aspirations, evolves based on their experiences.

Decline			
In adolescence:	In early adulthood:	In middle adulthood:	In late adulthood:
Giving less time to hobbies	Reducing sports participation	Focusing on essentials	Reducing working hours
Maintenance			
In adolescence:	In early adulthood:	In middle adulthood:	In late adulthood:
Verifying current occupational choice	Making occupational position secure	Holding one's own against competition	Keeping what one enjoys
Establishment			
In adolescence:	In early adulthood:	In middle adulthood:	In late adulthood:
Getting started in a chosen field	Settling down in a suitable position	Developing new skills	Doing things, one has wanted to do
Exploration			
In adolescence:	In early adulthood:	In middle adulthood:	In late adulthood:
Learning more about opportunities	Finding desired opportunity	Identifying new tasks to work on	Finding a good retirement place
Growth			
In adolescence:	In early adulthood:	In middle adulthood:	In late adulthood:
Developing a realistic self-concept	Learning to relate to others	Accepting one's own limitations	Developing and valuing non-occupational roles

Figure 4.1 Donald's Super Career Model

Source: Donald, 2012

Within this framework, reskilling becomes particularly important during the middle adulthood stage. As indicated in Figure 4.1, this is often the time when individuals engage in introspection and recalibration of their career paths, leading them to identify new domains where their skills can be applied. Upskilling, in contrast, is emphasized during early adulthood when individuals are intensely focused on establishing their career foundation. The process does not stop there—late adulthood often presents yet another opportunity for reskilling, allowing individuals to pursue long-deferred dreams and interests.

As we contemplate the future of work, the discourse often tends to focus on looming skill gaps and the urgent need for reskilling. While this is undeniably critical, it is equally important to design educational responses and workplace cultures that do more than just impart skills. They must also nurture the innate human capacities for creativity, problem-solving, and adaptability. The aim should be not just to produce workers who can do a job but to cultivate lifelong learners who can navigate the complexities of an ever-changing world. Skills, after all, are not just attributes; they are tickets to relevance in a continually evolving economic landscape.

Workplace skills are the essential building blocks that allow an individual to effectively perform job-related tasks and contribute meaningfully to their organization. These skills can be broadly categorized into four main types: technical skills, domain skills, behavioural skills, and functional skills. Technical skills serve as the bedrock of any job role; they are the specialized abilities needed to complete specific tasks. Domain skills, on the other hand, provide the contextual framework within which technical skills are applied. For instance, a computer programmer in the financial sector would not only need to be adept at coding but also have a nuanced understanding of banking regulations and processes.

Behavioural or soft skills, such as communication, planning, and teamwork, act as the glue that binds the technical and domain skills together, ensuring that tasks are not just completed, but also optimized for efficiency and impact. These soft skills often serve as transferable skills that can be applied across a variety of job roles and sectors, enhancing an individual's career flexibility and marketability.

According to Steve Scullen, an individual's skill set can be further divided into Technical Skills, Administrative Skills, Human Skills, and Citizenship Behaviours. Building upon this, Stuart Moss and David W. Hind in their book "Employability Skills," highlight additional competencies employers look for, such as oral and written communication, group collaboration, problem-solving, and data manipulation.

The dynamic nature of today's business landscape requires continuous adaptation and learning. Skills that were once in demand can quickly become obsolete, and new requirements continuously emerge. As a result, individuals must engage in perpetual self-assessment and learning to identify and acquire the skills that are in high demand. By doing so, they not only secure their current roles but also prepare themselves for future career opportunities.

The concept of "skilling" pertains to the training process that prepares individuals to perform specific tasks or jobs. The foundation for this trainability is initially established through formal education, which is subsequently supplemented by on-the-job training provided by employers. Companies not only focus on upskilling new recruits but also engage in regular performance assessments to identify upskilling opportunities for their existing workforce.

Skilling tends to divide into two distinct categories: social-cognitive skills associated with high-wage occupations and sensory-physical skills tied to low-wage jobs. Automation plays a dual role here; it boosts business productivity while also necessitating the transition of workers from low-skilled roles to higher-skilled, better-paying positions. However, this shift inevitably alters the skill sets needed to perform specific jobs.

The term "deskilling" refers to the simplification of jobs due to mechanization or computerization, to the extent that human expertise becomes less critical. As historian Adam Smith noted, deskilling emerged as an unintended consequence of the increasing division of labour, a trend that has been present since the dawn of industrialization. While it might reduce the need for certain skills, it concurrently elevates the demand for high-skilled workers in other sectors, leading to a constant need for "reskilling."

Reskilling is the act of acquiring new skills to perform a different job role or function. This often occurs when an employee seeks a promotion, transitions within an organization, or voluntarily shifts their career trajectory. With the advent of the Fourth Industrial Revolution (IR4.0), a large number of jobs are being transformed or even eliminated, while new roles are being created. This changing landscape makes reskilling crucial for the global workforce.

As illustrated in Figure 4.2, the skilling cycle is an ongoing process. It starts with initial "skilling" for job readiness, proceeds to "upskilling" for job enhancement, potentially moves to "deskilling" due to technological advancements, and eventually circles back to "reskilling" as job roles evolve or change entirely. This cycle perpetually turns, driven by constant shifts in industrial contexts and job requirements.

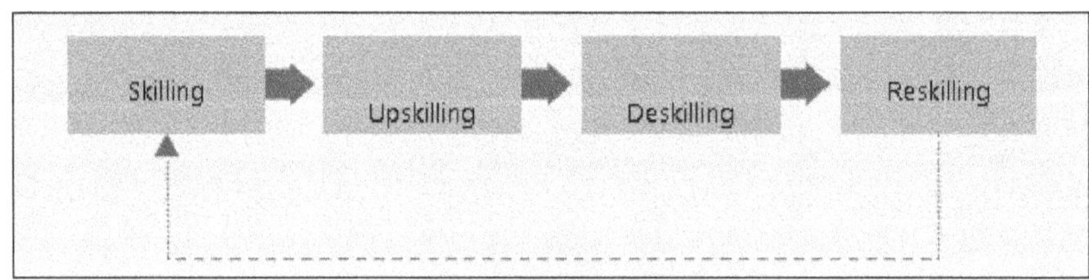

Figure 4.2 *Skilling Cycle*

Skill Acquisition and Self-skilling

The advent of Education 4.0 serves as an academic counterpart to the Fourth Industrial Revolution (IR4.0), preparing us for sweeping changes in the workforce. While formal education and training set the stage for acquiring job-related abilities, the journey toward mastering those skills is fundamentally self-directed. The concept of "Self-Skilling" focuses on individual initiatives to cultivate and refine new competencies.

In terms of theoretical underpinnings, Anderson's Skill Acquisition Theory outlines that learning a new skill traverses three cognitive stages: declarative, procedural, and automated learning. Dreyfus' model suggests that individuals advance through a hierarchy of skill levels—starting as novices and evolving into experts. According to Instance Theory, past experiences and the memory of specific instances significantly influence skill acquisition; practice naturally enhances performance over time.

The Model of Adaptive Control of Thought posits that adults begin acquiring new skills through explicit cognitive processes, and with adequate practice, transition to more implicit methods of learning. This human ability to learn complex skills sets us apart from other species and occurs over cognitive, associative, and autonomous stages, as informed by neural network models. These models suggest that knowledge is a network of weighted connections between processing units, and the patterns of these connections are strengthened through successive training trials.

In summary, the theories and frameworks surrounding skill acquisition emphasize that the learning of any skill is ultimately a responsibility that falls on the individual. While education and training can facilitate this process, the key driver in any skilling journey is the individual's own engagement in "learning."

Self-Skilling and Learning

Learning is characterized as a lasting alteration in the potential for behaviour, brought about through reinforced practice. Once learning has occurred, individuals exhibit new behaviours or capabilities that were not present prior to the learning experience. This change is not fleeting or static but enduring. The shift in behaviour might not manifest immediately after the learning event, but the potential for new behaviour is established, awaiting the right circumstances to be actualized. This transformation is facilitated through experiences or practices that are positively reinforced. A reinforcer, in this context, is any stimulus that naturally and spontaneously prompts a response from the individual undergoing the learning process.

From a Cognitive Learning Theory perspective, the mind actively engages with incoming information, processes it effectively, and then uses it to generate learning outcomes. In contrast, Skinner's Behaviourist Theory posits that learning is the result of a system of rewards and punishments, which can be either positive or negative. Vygotsky's Constructivist Theory offers another angle, advocating that learning is fundamentally a social process and that interactions with others are crucial for cognitive growth. The Humanist Theory of learning, meanwhile, focuses less on meeting predefined objectives and more on fulfilling an individual's potential.

As individuals mature, they increasingly assume agency over their own learning journey. This agency is particularly relevant in the context of reskilling and self-skilling, which are becoming increasingly crucial in today's rapidly changing work environment. The following sections will delve deeper into these critical aspects of learning, offering insights into the phenomena of reskilling and self-skilling.

▶ Adult Learning ◀

Malcolm Knowles pioneered the concept of adult learning, characterizing it as a journey of self-guided exploration. Generally, adults engage in the learning process with the intent to bring about some form of transformation, whether that involves acquiring new skills, altering behaviours, expanding knowledge, or shifting attitudes. Factors like the level of motivation, pre-existing knowledge, engagement in the learning process, and the application of learning outcomes differentiate adult learners from others. Adults typically bring their own set of preconceptions and emotional attitudes to the learning scenario, influenced by these factors.

Adult learners are usually goal-focused, keen on the relevance of the learning material, practical in their approach, and highly autonomous. They have an extensive base of previous experiences and knowledge that they bring into the learning environment, and they expect to be treated with respect. Various motivators drive adults to learn, including social connections (forming new friendships and associations), external expectations (meeting the recommendations of an authority figure), social well-being (enhancing one's ability to contribute to society), personal progression (seeking professional growth or higher job status), mental stimulation (breaking monotony or routine), and cognitive curiosity (learning for the sake of learning).

Andragogy, the science of adult learning, emphasizes the need for adults to take charge of their own learning experiences. Knowles, often referred to as the "father of andragogy," defined it as "the art and science of assisting adults in learning." This theory is constructed on six foundational principles: evolving self-concept, the value of prior experience, readiness for learning, a goal-oriented approach to learning, intrinsic motivation, and an immediate need to apply what is learned.

Self-Directed Learning (SDL)

Self-Directed Learning has garnered significant attention in the sphere of adult education and lifelong learning. With the digital revolution and the ubiquity of the internet, contemporary education systems have transformed, making knowledge accessible anytime and anywhere as required by the learner. In today's agile and flat organizational structures, the onus of learning is shifting increasingly toward the individual and the team, rather than being strictly controlled by the organization.

The importance of SDL is particularly pronounced in workplace learning, correlating positively with factors like internal locus of control, self-motivation, performance, self-confidence, and supportive environments. Originating from the realms of independent and non-formal adult learning, SDL is not just an educational trend but a fundamental human skill—the capacity to learn autonomously. It integrates a heightened sense of awareness about meaning and self-understanding as its core dimensions.

While the full potential of adult SDL is achieved by synthesizing external activities with internal contemplative aspects, the crux of SDL lies not in its sociological (independence in task management) or pedagogical (relevance in educational settings) facets but in its psychological or cognitive dimensions. Initial research on SDL was predominantly focused on its sociological and pedagogical aspects, with exceptions like Rogers (1969), who emphasized the learner's responsibility for their cognitive and motivational facets of learning. The ultimate aim lies in achieving cognitive liberty and mastering the art of "learning to learn."

Self-Regulated Learning

Self-Regulated Learning is defined by Zimmerman as "the systematic process where learners engage in and maintain thoughts, behaviours, and emotions geared towards achieving their objectives." Various models of Self-Regulated Learning (SRL) have been presented, each with different foundational theories. Zimmerman's own models are rooted in socio-cognitive theory, while Boekaerts' model emphasizes the role of objectives and emotions. Another model by Winne and Hadwin is framed within Information Processing Theory. Despite the different theoretical underpinnings, all these SRL models encompass cognitive, metacognitive, and motivational elements, as well as goal-setting mechanisms that propel the learning process forward.

To effectively support learners in becoming self-managed, it is vital to integrate an understanding of the self-managed learning process into any support structures. Feedback stands as a pivotal component in all SRL frameworks. In models like COPES, internal feedback occurs as learners assess their own progress against pre-defined goals. External feedback, on the other hand, can be administered by educators or other third-party entities to help in the self-management of learning.

Workplace Learning

In today's professional environment, a significant portion of learning is informal, self-initiated, and rooted in real-world scenarios. Elements like ongoing improvement, personal accountability, aligned values, exemplary leadership, embracing diversity, open communication, calculated risk-taking, collaboration, and innovation all contribute to fostering self-initiated learning at work. Management personnel often gain essential skills through self-guided education, hands-on training, and collaborative teamwork. Employees perceive workplace learning as a blend of self-guided observation, learning from mistakes, social interaction, formal instruction, leadership initiatives, strategic planning, and quality control. Both the demands of the job and an individual's orientation towards self-directed learning are key factors influencing learning behaviours in the workplace.

Formal and Informal Learning

Structured learning, either academic or vocational, occurs in a formalized setting such as a classroom or an online platform, and is guided by clearly laid-out goals and objectives typically set by an instructor. Hence, structured learning often relies on external guidance. Unstructured learning, conversely, is informal, based on experience, and happens outside traditional educational settings. It is often unintentional and takes place during daily interactions. Most skills are actually honed through this form of learning. Unstructured learning is often moderated by metacognitive understanding and self-regulation skills, facilitating the transfer of learned skills and knowledge. It stands as the predominant form of learning in professional settings.

Lifelong Learning

The concept of continual learning is a cultural shift that encourages both individuals and organizations to prioritize ongoing education. For lifelong learning to become integral to our lives, there must be new paradigms, physical spaces, organizational constructs, and incentive systems. These should enable individuals, collectives, and entire organizations to engage in risk-taking and innovation, as well as experiment with alternative learning paths. It is important to evaluate factors like motivation, interest, and community participation through long-term assessments. In the fast-changing job market, individuals, especially freelancers, must continually upgrade their skills. However, the relevance of skills is market-driven, so choosing what to learn is crucial. Artificial Intelligence can provide data-driven insights to guide learners in making informed career and learning decisions.

Self-Skilling and Motivation

Motivation is a complex interplay of factors that initiate and sustain targeted activities. Various theories attempt to explain motivation. Self-Determination Theory (SDT) posits that human beings have an inherent drive for competence, autonomy, and connectedness, making us naturally inclined to engage in learning and confront challenges. Vroom's Expectancy Value Theory suggests that motivation is directly proportional to the perceived chances of success and the value attached to that success. Attribution Theory focuses on the explanations individuals create for their successes or failures, affecting their level of motivation. In the Social Cognitive Theory, self-efficacy is considered the main catalyst for motivated actions, while Goal Orientation Theory asserts that motivation is driven by the pursuit of mastery over a particular subject.

Research in self-skilling has linked motivation as a key determinant. Factors such as extrinsic rewards, external controls, and feedback can significantly influence one's intrinsic motivation for self-directed learning. Motivation plays a central role in facilitating learners to take ownership and control of their educational journey. The "Two-Shells-Model of Motivated Self-Directed Learning" provides a framework where continuous motivation for intentional learning is dynamically shaped by the outcomes of actual learning experiences. This, in turn, influences the design of learning environments that further foster self-direction. Instructional methods, including lectures and feedback, can inspire a greater degree of self-directed learning. Models like Keller's ARCS have been used to design technology-assisted instructional methods that enhance motivation for self-directed learning. Ultimately, self-directed learning is a foundational skill for lifelong education and is significantly impacted by factors like motivation, metacognition, and self-regulation. Research has shown strong correlations between self-efficacy, learning motivation, and self-directed learning, all of which significantly influence problem-solving skills. Intrinsic motivation, self-directed learning, and performance are intrinsically linked, as are self-efficacy, motivation, and cognitive strategies.

Re-skilling Outcomes

Ensuring positive outcomes for individuals undergoing upskilling or reskilling is essential across all industry sectors. However, the roadmap to effective reskilling often remains ambiguous, given the unpredictability of future skill benefits and the evolving nature of new technological demands. While the incremental value of mastering a new skill is largely influenced by one's existing skill set, branching out to different domains often boosts job prospects and addresses talent gaps. Reconfiguring skills in innovative combinations can yield significant benefits, especially for roles like Data Scientists.

The emergence of digital learning platforms has fostered the creation of novel job roles by merging diverse skill sets. Given the balance of costs and advantages associated with acquiring new skills, decisions regarding reskilling are intricate and unique to each individual. Analysing data from digital learning platforms and freelancing portals can provide insights into the synergies of acquiring specific skills, aiding in the identification of sustainable, personalized, and lucrative reskilling paths.

By employing continuous-time series analysis of multi-skilling trajectories using platform data, one can offer tailored recommendations on the merits of acquiring a particular skill in an ever-evolving tech landscape. Such insights can mitigate employment mismatches. Reskilling plays a pivotal role in providing a safety net for workers facing economic challenges, enhancing their capacity to both benefit from and drive productivity. It can facilitate global trade, better position workers in the employment landscape, ensure improved salaries, working environments, and productivity levels, and pave the way for career progression and in-house promotions. Both organizations and their employees stand to gain immensely from effective reskilling.

Adult learners are often driven by tangible results, such as career advancements, compared to younger learners. The aspiration for tangible outcomes, like securing a more rewarding job, plays a pivotal role in maintaining an adult's engagement and perseverance in the workforce. Hence, it is crucial that lifelong learning structures align with the specific needs of local employers.

Recent studies indicate that technical and vocational education models can significantly boost earnings and further educational pursuits. These models offer two distinct advantages. Firstly, they often present numerous active learning opportunities since they are tailored to real-world job tasks.

Secondly, they align training with the burgeoning demands of industries. Implementing sector-specific strategies, where training programs are deliberately aligned with labour market needs, has proven to yield positive results in job placements and salary increments. This underscores the importance of not just amplifying career guidance but also equipping both job seekers and training providers with the tools to pinpoint promising and emergent job sectors and maximize workers' existing skill sets to tap into these opportunities.

Investing in reskilling current employees brings multifaceted advantages to an organization. Workers feel a sense of security, knowing that they would not be sidelined if they embrace reskilling initiatives. For employers, retaining and nurturing existing talent enhances their contribution to the company's growth. This fostered loyalty and heightened commitment not only uplifts the team spirit but also fosters a culture of innovation within the company. Moreover, the cost of upskilling and reskilling existing employees is often more economical than the expenses tied to hiring and training new personnel.

In this book, self-skilling is explored as a facet of adult learning. To discern how it can be effectively harnessed to reskill employees within organizations, a deep dive into the existing theories and models prevalent in adult learning research is essential. Insights drawn from previously discussed theories related to skill acquisition, learning, and motivation shed light on the nuances of self-skilling. Building on these insights, the subsequent section will outline and introduce the new Employee Self-Skilling Model ESSM®, that elucidates the factors associated with employee self-skilling and their influence on reskilling outcomes within any organization.

Self-Determination Theory

Deci&Ryan'sSelf-determinationtheory(SDT)delvesintothemotivational aspects of personality, development, and societal interactions. It scrutinizes how varying social environments and individual variances influence different forms of motivation, subsequently affecting learning outcomes, performance, and overall psychological well-being.

At the heart of SDT lie three fundamental human needs: Competence, Autonomy, and Relatedness. Meeting these needs is vital for optimal human functioning and well-being. When these needs are met, they foster autonomous motivation and intrinsic aspirations, leading individuals to naturally regulate their behaviour and harbour an innate drive to learn and embrace challenges. Over the years, SDT has gained significant traction and has been rigorously applied in the realm of self-directed learning.

Theory of Reasoned Action

Fishbein and Ajzen's theory of reasoned action (TRA) stands as a cornerstone in the realm of social psychology, providing profound insights into human behaviour. This theory has long been regarded as a crucial model for understanding intentional human actions. TRA postulates that an individual's behaviour is shaped by intentions, which in turn are influenced by their attitudes towards the behaviour and by subjective norms.

An individual's attitude reflects their sentiments, either positive or negative, towards executing a specific behaviour. This attitude is formed based on the individual's beliefs regarding the outcomes of that behaviour and their evaluation of these outcomes. On the other hand, subjective norms revolve around an individual's perception of the opinions held by key figures in their life, such as family, peers, authority figures, and media. Over the years, TRA has been extensively applied and rigorously assessed in the domains of Self-directed learning, eLearning, and mLearning.

Theory of Planned Behaviour

Ajzen's Theory of Planned Behaviour (TPB) evolved from the foundational Theory of Reasoned Action (TRA), serving as a refined extension of it. TPB stands out as one of the predominant theories in understanding and predicting human actions. While TRA primarily focuses on intention, TPB broadens this by introducing an added dimension, known as perceived behavioural control (PBC). TPB posits that an individual's actions are a direct outcome of both PBC and behavioural intention (BI).

In this theory, behavioural intentions, which serve as indicators of an individual's readiness to act in a certain way, are shaped by three distinct elements: attitude, subjective norms, and perceived behavioural control. While attitude reflects an individual's overall appraisal (positive or negative) about enacting a specific behaviour, subjective norms encapsulate the perceived pressures or expectations from significant others. Perceived behavioural control, on the other hand, gauges one's self-assessment of their capability to execute a behaviour, taking into account available resources and potential obstacles.

Diving deeper, these primary constructs are underpinned by core belief systems: attitudinal beliefs (estimations about potential outcomes of a behaviour), normative beliefs (perceptions about societal expectations), and control beliefs (perceptions about the degree of personal control over a behaviour). TPB, with its enriched framework, offers a more nuanced understanding of the determinants of intention and subsequent behaviour. It has found substantial application and empirical validation, especially in the realm of self-directed learning.

Technology Acceptance Model

Technology Acceptance Model (TAM) stands as a pivotal framework in Information System (IS) research. Originating from the Theory of Reasoned Action (TRA), the TAM focuses on determining a user's inclination towards adopting a particular technology. Tailored specifically for the IS domain, TAM aims to forecast the acceptance and utilization of information technology within organizations. This model emphasizes intention as a critical factor, linking it directly to actual usage. It comprises five central constructs: perceived usefulness, perceived ease of use, attitude towards usage, intention to use, and actual use. The model asserts that user acceptance of technology is primarily influenced by two perceptions: the perceived ease of use and the perceived usefulness of the technology. Davis describes perceived usefulness as the extent to which an individual believes that using a particular system will enhance their performance. On the other hand, perceived ease of use refers to an individual's belief regarding the user-friendliness and simplicity of a system. Intentions to use the technology are shaped by the user's attitude, influenced both directly and indirectly by their perceptions of ease of use and usefulness.

In the given model, the crucial predictors of technology usage are perceived usefulness and perceived ease of use. Within this structure, the only direct influencer of actual usage is the behavioural intention. There are two primary reasons for positioning intention as an intermediary variable: firstly, the intention to undertake an action is generally seen as a precursor to the action itself, and secondly, the inclusion of intention enhances the model's predictive capability. The model envisions external factors affecting intentions and usage through perceived usefulness and perceived ease of use.

Taylor & Todd further evolved this model into the Decomposed Theory of Planned Behaviour (DTPB) by integrating additional elements and expanding upon TPB. Here, foundational beliefs such as attitude, normative beliefs, and control beliefs are further dissected into multifaceted constructs. Drawing from the Diffusion of Innovation theory, three pivotal characteristics of an innovation—relative advantage, complexity, and compatibility—are incorporated to guide its adoption. Relative advantage mirrors the TAM's "perceived usefulness," while complexity aligns with "perceived ease of use." Compatibility gauges how well an innovation aligns with existing values, needs, and past experiences of potential adopters.

Furthermore, the DTPB dissects subjective norms into peer and superior influences, and perceived behavioural control splits into self-efficacy and facilitating conditions. These facilitating conditions, seen as essential resources to execute a behaviour, branch out into resource-related and technology-related conditions. Self-efficacy pertains to one's confidence in successfully executing a particular behaviour under specified circumstances. DTPB provides a comprehensive and nuanced understanding, making it a more potent tool in deciphering IT adoption intentions compared to its foundational models.

Furthermore, TAM has been extensively applied and empirically evaluated in the realm of technology-driven, self-directed learning platforms.

Social Cognitive Theory (SCT)

Bandura's Social Cognitive Theory (SCT) stands as a cornerstone for understanding individual behaviour. SCT serves as a guiding structure, dissecting human motivation, cognition, and actions, presenting a model where environment, personal factors, and behaviour interact dynamically. The theory posits that individual actions are shaped by both societal influences and personal cognition.

Two vital cognitive components driving behaviour are self-efficacy expectations and outcome expectations. While outcome expectancy pertains to an individual's belief about the outcomes of certain behaviours, self-efficacy revolves around the confidence in one's ability to execute actions leading to those outcomes. SCT emphasizes the role of beliefs in guiding actions, irrespective of perceived outcomes. It suggests that psychological mechanisms adjust personal efficacy expectations, which subsequently impact one's choice of actions, effort level, perseverance, and approach to challenges. As per SCT, self-directed learning (SDL) is moulded by individual, environmental, and behavioural factors. This theory has found extensive application and correlation in the domain of SDL research.

Skill Acquisition Theory

This theory delves into the evolution of individuals as they acquire and master new abilities. Based on foundational principles, it addresses the learning of both cognitive and psychomotor skills across diverse scenarios, from classroom settings to sports or industrial environments. The theory outlines three distinct phases of skill development, each marked by notable variations in knowledge acquisition and application.

Initially, learners garner knowledge by keenly observing others performing the skill or by listening to experts share their insights. This stage involves the accumulation of declarative knowledge, which is stored as fragmented information in memory. As learners progress to the next phase, they start to convert this knowledge into actionable behaviour, known as procedural knowledge. This stage sees learners storing information as patterns or sequences, enabling them to easily retrieve and replicate the desired action.

With consistent practice, learners transition to the final stage, achieving a state of automaticity. Here, knowledge becomes so ingrained that performing the skill becomes instinctive, requiring minimal conscious thought and yielding fewer mistakes.

While certain activities, especially those emphasizing motor functions or repetitive work tasks, thrive on this automatic retrieval of procedural knowledge, some tasks necessitate the integration of both declarative and procedural knowledge. Over-practicing, or overlearning, might not always be beneficial in such scenarios. For optimal efficiency in varied situations, a balance between well-ingrained procedural knowledge and robust, adaptable declarative knowledge is crucial, especially when faced with unfamiliar contexts.

Theory of Self-Directed Learning

The SDLRS, or Self-Directed Learning Readiness Scale, offers a tool to gauge an individual's self-assessed competencies and mindset related to self-directed learning. This scale is built upon eight key attributes and personality traits that are indicative of one's inclination towards self-directedness. Beyond just assessing one's preparedness for self-directed learning, the SDLRS is employed to explore correlations between readiness for self-directed learning and various personal attributes.

The assessment consists of 58 statements, with responses measured on a 5-point scale, from "always true" to "never true". Out of these, 41 are framed positively while 17 have a negative connotation. Furthermore, for wider accessibility, the tool has been translated into multiple languages. The SDLRS has seen extensive application in educational research.

Refer to Table 4.1 for a comprehensive overview of the primary theories and models related to understanding the concept of self-skilling.

Table 4.1 *Key Theories / Frameworks for Understanding Self-Skilling*

Model/Theory	Author(s)	Brief Description
Self-determination theory	Deci & Ryan	Human beings have a natural tendency to develop autonomous regulation of behaviour and are intrinsically motivated to learn and take on challenges
Theory of Reasoned Action	Fishbein & Ajzen	Human behaviour is driven by intentions that are built based on the individual's attitude towards the behaviour and upon subjective norms
Theory of Planned Behaviour	Ajzen	Individual behaviour is a direct function of perceived behavioural control (PBC) and behavioural intention (BI)
Technology Acceptance Model	Davis	Perceived usefulness and Perceived ease of use are the primary drivers of new technology acceptance
Theory of Self-directed Learning	Guglielmino	The Self-Directed Learning Readiness Scale, or SDLRS, is a method for evaluating an individual's perception of their skills and attitudes that are associated with self-directedness in learning.
Theory of skill acquisition	DeKeyser	This theory explains how people progress in learning new skills and gain advanced proficiencies.
Social Cognitive Theory	Bandura	The two major cognitive forces, which influence an individual behaviour, are self- efficacy expectations and outcome expectations.

CHAPTER – 5

Leveraging Self-Skilling for Reskilling using Employee Self-Skilling Model (ESSM)®

Before diving into this chapter, let us clarify some key terms to ensure we are all on the same wavelength. The term 'Skill' is the practical ability to perform a task, rather than just knowing about it. 'Skilling' is the process of training to execute a specific task or job. 'Upskilling' involves enhancing work efficiency and capabilities through further training. 'Deskilling' refers to automating or computerizing a task to the extent that minimal human intervention is needed. 'Reskilling' is about acquiring new skills to take on a different job or retraining for a different role. Lastly, 'Self-Skilling' pertains to individuals' efforts to independently develop and refine their knowledge and abilities.

Importance of Self-Skilling

By 2025, it is projected that employers will prioritize reskilling and upskilling for roughly 70% of their workforce. Yet, research indicates that only about 40% of workers actively participate and successfully complete employer-sponsored reskilling programs. Some reskilling initiatives demand time away from work or acquiring new formal credentials, which can be daunting for those who have been away from academic settings for years.

The journey of continuous learning and adaptation is not straightforward, and individuals need adequate support and motivation to envision the long-term rewards of such endeavours. A more transparent, data-informed approach could offer clarity and options for these workers. The overarching goal is to foster a mindset in individuals that embraces adaptability, curiosity, and lifelong learning in a constantly evolving world. The World Bank G20 Report in 2016 emphasized that to stay employable in the future landscape, we need to anticipate dynamic skill demands and evolve policies that accentuate on-the-job training, workplace flexibility, and labour fluidity. The pivot to a large-scale career transition and nationwide reskilling hinges heavily on individual determination and perspective. Their role cannot be understated.

Why Self-Skilling?

There are numerous factors emphasizing the significance of individual self-skilling endeavours amidst the ongoing reskilling evolution. Let us delve into these to understand more.

Adult Learning Theories

Theories on adult learning emphasize learner independence, active participation in processing shared knowledge, and the importance of reflection. For over thirty years, the principles of self-directed learning have been the backbone of Adult Education. A review of scholarly articles indicates that there are over 200 terminologies associated with self-directed learning. It is theorized that the heightened interest, especially in Western countries, correlates with their cultural emphasis on independence and autonomy.

Embedding the habit of self-directed learning from a young age can optimize lifelong learning. Jarvis, in 1992, highlighted the importance of fostering autonomy and the exercise of free will, associating autonomy with adulthood and free will with democratic values. Wang and Canton's 2014 research posited that self-directed learning remains a potent tool for learning throughout life.

With technological advancements, there has been a surge in literature and tools promoting self-directed learning, aiming to enhance learner independence. Thus, adult learning theories underscore that harnessing the power of self-skilling amidst the reskilling movement is pivotal for preparing individuals, businesses, sectors, and nations to cultivate a flexible workforce.

Advent of Technology in Learning

The modern era's unparalleled connectivity and easy access to information have significantly simplified self-directed learning. The rise of eLearning and edtech has been monumental, with a plethora of courses available at the click of a button. Beyond formal courses, the internet is awash with expert insights, open-access journals, podcasts, tutorials, and interactive forums that cater to immediate learning needs. Many online communities engage in collaborative learning, discussing topics and sharing knowledge. This vast repository of knowledge, coupled with tools and platforms tailored for eLearning, empowers learners to navigate their education at their own convenience.

The COVID-19 pandemic further catalysed the self-skilling movement. Global lockdowns and home confinement turned DIY (Do-It-Yourself) activities from optional hobbies to essential skills. Many found themselves mastering new abilities, from domestic chores like cooking and haircutting to using video conferencing tools and remotely managing teams. Both the pandemic's limitations and evolving business requirements accelerated the adoption of tech-driven platforms for self-learning. Consequently, there was a notable surge in individuals pursuing online learning opportunities—four times the usual rate. Similarly, government learning program enrolments saw a nine-fold rise, while employers recorded a five-fold boost in offering online learning opportunities to their employees.

In 2020, the eLearning market value exceeded 250 billion USD, with projections indicating an impressive CAGR of over 21% from 2021 to 2027. The surge in this domain will be propelled by cutting-edge technologies such as Artificial Intelligence, Virtual Reality, and cloud computing, all contributing to the creation of intelligent content, digital study materials, and real-time interactive tools (source: Gminsights. com). The eLearning platforms have witnessed a remarkable rise in both academic and corporate sectors over the past few years. The COVID-19 pandemic further reshaped this landscape.

UNESCO reported that, as of March 2020, school closures impacted over 1.2 billion students across 186 countries, leading to a significant spike in distance learning registrations worldwide. Cloud-based solutions empower learners with anytime, anywhere access to content, while institutions can set up virtual spaces for both educators and students. Additionally, these technologies ensure heightened data protection for institutions and secure online transactions. With immersive technologies, communication and collaboration have been enhanced, enriching the overall learning experience for students and professionals alike. The competitive eLearning landscape is prompting new entrants to innovate continuously, fortifying their market stance.

Identifying the ideal knowledge source can be daunting, but it is equally crucial to recognize that in our rapidly evolving world, individuals can not solely rely on external guidance for their educational paths. As we head into an era marked by incessant change, not only will there be a push for innovative ideas and products, but individuals will also need to continually reshape their skills to stay pertinent and competitive.

The upcoming landscape necessitates the cultivation of perpetual learners who can autonomously seek and absorb new knowledge and skills throughout their careers. As we transition from agricultural to industrial economies, there is an emphasis on nurturing knowledgeable workers proficient in data analysis and critical thinking. A hundred years ago, most children globally underwent less than five years of formal education. However, with the advent of industrialization and the subsequent demand for a skilled workforce, this duration has expanded to nearly 15 years in many nations. Given the lengthening human lifespan and shifting job dynamics, individuals now enjoy extended careers with frequent job transitions.

The Fourth Industrial Revolution introduces us to a realm dominated by automation and AI. Due to these upheavals across social, economic, and tech domains, the formal education received in our early years is no longer sufficient for lifelong sustenance. As a result, continuous learning and post-formal education become essential. With Education 4.0 aligning with the principles of Industrial Revolution(IR) 4.0, there are abundant opportunities for continual education. Numerous eLearning platforms have teamed up with prestigious universities, offering a chance not just to acquire new skills but also to attain advanced qualifications, ensuring individuals remain valuable contributors to the economy. These tech platforms cater to various online learning needs.

Individual Courses – These courses focus on a specific topic and are characterized by their standalone nature. Completion durations can range from a few weeks to several months.

Course Bundles – Many online education platforms offer grouped courses for a comprehensive understanding of a subject area. On various platforms, these are termed as Nanodegrees, Specializations, or Learning Tracks.

Undergraduate Degrees – Platforms such as EdX and Coursera collaborate with universities to provide formal bachelor's degrees online. Though these might cost up to $15,000, they generally offer a more affordable alternative to traditional on-campus programs from the same institutions.

Postgraduate Degrees – Similarly, platforms like EdX, Coursera, and UpGrad partner with universities to offer recognized master's degree programs online.

Specialized Topics – Certain platforms specialize in particular domains. For instance, Datacamp concentrates on data science, Creative Live targets creative disciplines such as photography and design, and Pluralsight and Code Academy cater primarily to software developers.

The diversity in platforms is evident in their offerings. For instance, Udemy, Coursera, and LinkedIn Learning provide courses in multiple languages, including Spanish, German, and Portuguese. While niche platforms foster vibrant communities for collaborative learning experiences. Pricing structures also differ among platforms; Udemy charges per course, Skill Share and LinkedIn Learning operate on a subscription basis, whereas Coursera and Edx present an array of options ranging from per course charges to fees for specializations or degrees. Course completion methods also differ: some platforms rely on self-assessment, others employ peer reviews, and a few mandate exams for certification. Content quality varies too; for instance, Udacity collaborates with industry giants like Google for content creation, while Edx and Coursera source their material from leading universities. Niche platforms such as Creative Live, Pluralsight, and Datacamp are recognized for high-quality offerings within their focus areas. Table 5.1 outlines notable eLearning platforms with their distinct value propositions, while Table 5.2 details their pricing models and user demographics (sourced from www.elearningindustry.com).

These eLearning platforms have gained immense popularity globally. Although India boasts a vast audience for online education, limited providers cater to the working demographic. Most homegrown eLearning platforms, including Byju, Vedantu, myCBSEguide, Merit Nation, Vidyakul, Toppr, and Unacademy, are oriented towards school students or those preparing for competitive examinations. According to reports by Meity and Elearning Industry, there is a noticeable gap in indigenous solutions for working professionals in India.

Though online educational platforms empower self-directed learners to gain essential knowledge for specific tasks or roles, the transition from theoretical understanding to practical application and achieving expertise through consistent practice often remains unaddressed. Recognizing the need for new skills and the potential of self-skilling is one aspect, but the true measure of these transformative paths lies in the successful application of acquired knowledge. While tech-driven learning platforms provide ample scope for explicit learning crucial for skill development, they often overlook the implicit learning aspect. Implicit learning, which is more intuitive and unspoken, plays a vital role in the overall skilling journey. A comprehensive study of self-skilling and reskilling must encompass the unique nuances of this implicit learning experience for each individual.

The Quantum of Re-skilling Need and its Impact.

The total working-age population across 26 primary global economies stands at 2713 million. As indicated in Table 5.3, India ranks second, following China, in terms of its working-age population. The mean labour force engagement rate is approximately 65.72% (translating to about 1783 million individuals). This data suggests that roughly 34% or 922 million people of the working-age demographic, rely on the remaining active workforce. Among these 26 nations, India exhibits the second-lowest active labour participation rate, resulting in a higher count of dependent individuals. Nevertheless, India boasts the second-largest actively working population (326 million) globally, surpassed only by China with 580 million participants. Unless individuals take active interest in reskilling themselves such a large-scale workforce transformation may take several years.

Vulnerable Employment

Vulnerable employment encompasses individuals who are self-employed, run their own businesses, or work in family enterprises. Figure 5.1 illustrates the global distribution of employment based on its status. From this figure, it is evident that the Asia-Pacific region leads in terms of employment numbers. However, a significant 37% of these workers are self-employed, with another 11% contributing to family businesses, and 3% being employers.

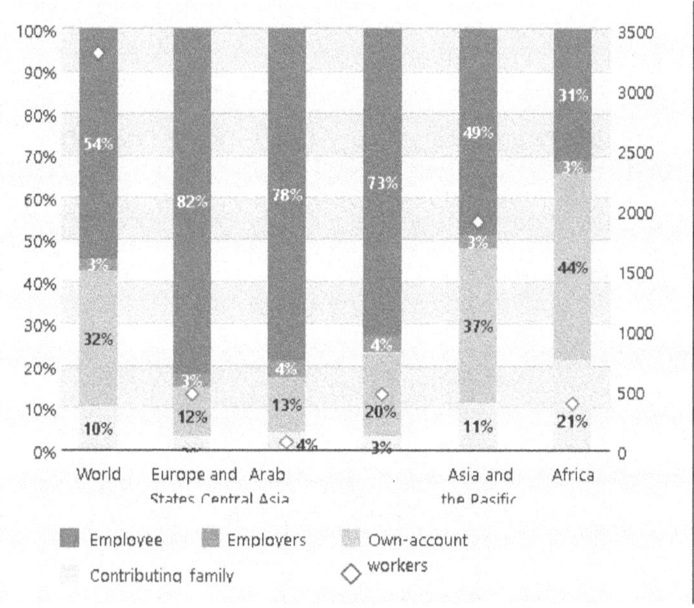

Figure 5.1 Vulnerable Employment Status

Source: https://ilostat.ilo.org

Only 49% are employed in formal organizations. In contrast, in Europe and Central Asia, a vast 82% of the workforce is part of organizational structures. When comparing regions, it is evident that Africa, Asia, and the Pacific have a significant percentage of their workforce in vulnerable employment, in contrast to Europe, Arab States, and the Americas, which predominantly have their workforce in organizations. Globally, only 54% of workers are in formal organizations, with the rest falling under the vulnerable employment category. Hence, any reskilling initiative should be designed to cater not only to those in formal sectors but also to a significant percentage that falls outside of it, ensuring employability is not compromised.

India, in particular, has a startlingly high rate of vulnerable employment. Its rate of vulnerable employment, at 74%, is considerably higher than the 20% average across the 26 analyzed countries (sourced from ilostat.ilo.org). This highlights the pressing need for India's reskilling efforts to be expansive and cater to those who manage their own career progression and skill enhancement.

Short Supply of Skills Required to Business

Businesses worldwide are facing a noticeable skill deficit. On average, businesses find that only 58.5% of the needed skills are available, and this percentage dips to a concerning 42.3% for India. Companies globally have highlighted challenges in hiring due to the dearth of suitable talent and find existing strategies insufficient to bridge this talent chasm. Individuals play a pivotal role in addressing this skill mismatch.

They need to be forward-looking, grasp overarching trends, and delineate the steps necessary for personal skill enhancement and adaptability. Entrusting individuals with the responsibility of their own reskilling can expedite the process of meeting skill demands more effectively and broadly.

Digital Dexterity Among Active Population

Across all nations, 59.5% of the workforce possesses digital skills. India stands in the middle ground with 49.2% of its active population having digital proficiency. Utilizing technology-driven education can not only hasten the reskilling of the workforce but also facilitate this change at a larger scale. The digital capability of the workforce can empower countries to maximize these tech-centred training tools for their upskilling missions.

Nevertheless, the essence of self-motivation is profound in tech-based education, underscoring the learner's proactive involvement and self-improvement aptitudes. Given that a significant portion of today's workforce comprises digital natives, coupled with the rise of tech-anchored learning platforms globally, it becomes essential to assess the potential of tapping into the digital savvy of the populace for upskilling and reskilling endeavours.

Sentiments of Employers

Foremost, the predominant reaction from employers worldwide to the evolving skill demands is to anticipate that their employees will acquire the necessary skills on the job, alongside considering the retraining of current staff and potential work automation. Across all nations, the primary method chosen by employers to facilitate reskilling is through their internal learning and development departments. It is clear that employer sentiments lean towards expecting employees to shoulder the responsibility and take initiative in self-skilling. Table 5.3 provides a summary of employer perspectives from various countries, highlighting their national profiles, primary responses to changing skill needs, and their leading projected avenues for reskilling.

Training Transfer on the Job

Self-skilling is deeply intertwined with the process of acquiring new job-related abilities. The learning journey does not truly conclude with just the acquisition of new knowledge; it is only fulfilled when this knowledge is practically applied and refined into a skill for a specific role, and when proficiency in that skill is honed through repeated practice. Here, the individual takes centre stage in the skill acquisition phase.

A key trait for the modern workforce is fluid intelligence, which reflects one's adaptability and speed in processing knowledge, learning, and devising innovative solutions to challenges. Defined as the capability to reason and dynamically handle novel information, fluid intelligence is crucial in today's evolving work environment, with individuals primarily responsible for cultivating and sharpening this trait.

Empowering individuals with the tools for self-skilling is a long-term solution for workforce reskilling, both now and in the future. Those proficient in self-skilling stand to benefit most from reskilling initiatives, ensuring they remain pertinent and continually deliver value to their organizations.

Table 5.1: *Top Self-Skilling Platforms*

Source: Websites

Platform	Best suited for
Udacity	Individuals who are looking to professionally develop or have a career change. Helps in finding suiTable jobs for learners.
Courserra	Students wanting the highest quality education and looking to earn accredited completion certificates and university diplomas.
Skillshare	Professionals that are not bothered about getting accomplishment certificates but want to keep on improving their skills or learn new skills at an affordable cost.
Masterclass	Anyone looking for motivation or inspiration on the creative and exciting topics like Food or Wellness. A VIP or celebrity teaches learners.
Datacomp	Beginners or someone looking to develop their skills in Data Science and Analytics
Udemy	Those prefer to pay for each course individually and have access for life. It is also an affordable platform, but one needs to do a due diligence to assess course quality.
Edx	Anyone looking to earn accredited certificates or university degrees.

Platform	Best suited for
LinkedIn Learning	Those who are looking for a huge pool of good content for a (relatively) small annual subscription. Added value for intensive social media users (particularly LinkedIn).
Pluralsight	Those looking for high-quality courses in technology related topics and a decent size library of courses.
Brilliant	Anyone who enjoys problem-solving and hands on learning. Its courses are designed for Students, Professionals and Lifelong learners who can all benefit in some way from this platform. Those looking to master a STEM topic or just want to keep the mind active, there is something for everyone.
Code academy	Learning coding with many of its courses being beginner friendly and self-paced
Creative Live	Creatives and innovators with courses taught by experienced and handpicked instructors.
Mind valley	Those looking for personal growth and transformation
treehouse	Someone who is looking to gain tech skills in subjects like web design, web development, mobile development and more. Many of its courses are designed with beginners in mind.
Simplilearn	Like edX or Coursera, those looking for good-quality courses and the possibility to earn an official certificate, should consider Simplilearn.

Table 5.2 *Pricing Plans of Self-Skilling Platforms*

Source: upskillwise.com

Platform	Annual price	Monthly price	Number of courses	Certificates
Skillshare	$167.88	No monthly option	35,000+	No
LinkedIn Learning	~$239.98	$29.99	16,000+	Yes, not accredited
Coursera Plus	–	$59 a month	3,000+	Yes
MasterClass	$180	$15 monthly instalments available	100+	No

Code academy	~$239.98	$39.99	1,800 hours of content in IT	No
Pluralsight Personal	Personal: $299	$29	2,500+	No
Pluralsight Premium	Premium: $449	$45	7,000+	Yes, not accredited
Creative Live	Creator Pass: $149 ($12.42/ month)	$15 a month (annual commitment billed annually) $39	2,000+ creative courses	No
Datacamp	Standard: $300	$25 month billed annually	350+	Statements of Accomplishment
Standard Data camp Premium	Premium: $399	$33.25 a month billed annually		

Table 5.3: *Country Profiles and Top Responses to Shifting Needs*

Source: J. Brown et al., 2017; Forum, 2020; Lund et al., 2021

Country	Working Age Population	Labour force participation	Vulnerable Employment	Supply of business relevant skills	Digital Skills among active population	Top Response to Shifting Skill needs	Top projected use of training providers
Argentina	1,76,40,048	65.70%	21.90%	54%	50.10%	Retrain existing employees	Internal learning and development
Australia	1,73,32,023	65.60%	10.60%	59.70%	65.50%	Retrain existing employees	Internal learning and development
Brazil	13,61,54,622	64.20%	27.90%	42.20%	36.90%	Look to automate work	Internal learning and development

Country	Working Age Population	Labour force participation	Vulnerable Employment	Supply of business relevant skills	Digital Skills among active population	Top Response to Shifting Skill needs	Top projected use of training providers
Canada	2,63,59,853	65.90%	10.70%	68.40%	67.90%	Retrain existing employees	Internal learning and development
China	78,40,00,000	74.00%	45.10%	71.10%	71.70%	Expect existing employees to pick up skills on the job	Internal learning and development
France	4,59,68,569	58.40%	7.40%	55.90%	57.10%	Retrain existing employees	Internal learning and development
Germany	6,22,81,725	63.30%	5.60%	60.80%	62.50%	Expect existing employees to pick up skills on the job	Internal learning and development
India	58,83,73,756	55.50%	74%	42.30%	49.20%	Expect existing employees to pick up skills on the job	Internal learning and development
Indonesia	15,30,09,507	74.00%	47.50%	61%	60.60%	Look to automate work	Internal learning and development

Country	Working Age Population	Labour force participation	Vulnerable Employment	Supply of business relevant skills	Digital Skills among active population	Top Response to Shifting Skill needs	Top projected use of training providers
Italy	4,61,22,130	52.90%	16.90%	52.30%	50.70%	Look to automate work	Internal learning and development
Japan	9,87,10,000	63.70%	8.30%	52.90%	50.80%	Expect existing employees to pick up skills on the job	Internal learning and development
Malaysia	1,62,31,000	77.60%	21.70%	64.40%	66.30%	Look to automate work	Internal learning and development
Mexico	7,30,69,000	64.60%	26.90%	50.50%	42.90%	Retrain existing employees	Internal learning and development
Netherlands	1,22,36,238	63.90%	12.60%	63.70%	77.40%	Expect existing employees to pick up skills on the job	Internal learning and development
Pakistan	8,23,45,263	56.30%	55.30%	51.10%	50.70%	Retrain existing employees	Internal learning and development
Poland	2,67,45,715	59.00%	15.90%	52.70%	55.60%	Expect existing employees to pick up skills on the job	Internal learning and development

Country	Working Age Population	Labour force participation	Vulnerable Employment	Supply of business relevant skills	Digital Skills among active population	Top Response to Shifting Skill needs	Top projected use of training providers
Russian Federation	10,69,13,416	66.10%	5.30%	59.20%	66%	Expect existing employees to pick up skills on the job	Internal learning and development
Saudi Arabia	2,05,18,278	64.40%	3%	71%	73.90%	Expect existing employees to pick up skills on the job	Internal learning and development
Singapore	29,38,300	73.00%	9.70%	69.10%	77%	Expect existing employees to pick up skills on the job	Internal learning and development
South Africa	3,16,27,389	64.90%	10.30%	44.40%	29.90%	Look to automate work	Internal learning and development
Spain	3,50,92,188	61.20%	11%	59.70%	55.20%	Retrain existing employees	Internal learning and development
Switzerland	63,26,839	68.50%	8.90%	62.70%	72%	Look to automate work	Internal learning and development

Country	Working Age Population	Labour force participation	Vulnerable Employment	Supply of business relevant skills	Digital Skills among active population	Top Response to Shifting Skill needs	Top projected use of training providers
Thailand	4,72,15,919	72.20%	48.20%	53.60%	54.90%	Expect existing employees to pick up skills on the job	Internal learning and development
United Arab Emirates	81,12,786	85.20%	0.90%	70.50%	71.70%	Expect existing employees to pick up skills on the job	Internal learning and development
United Kingdom	4,63,80,358	64.30%	12.90%	58.60%	61%	Retrain existing employees	Internal learning and development
United States	22,14,26,962	64.30%	3.80%	69.70%	69.40%	Retrain existing employees	Internal learning and development

Employee Self-Skilling Model(ESSM)® for Reskilling Employees Within Organizations

Within any organization, employees continually self-skill as they adapt to their designated tasks. This principle is equally applicable during their reskilling phases when they transition to a different role. The Employee Self-Skilling Model(ESSM)® provides an evidence-based framework to harness self-skilling during employee reskilling processes within companies. It elucidates the elements tied to employee self-skilling and the interplay among these components. ESSM® has been empirically evaluated through extensive assessment of employee self-skilling behaviours across multiple organizations.

As depicted in the accompanying illustration, the ESSM® identifies twelve elements linked to the process of Employee Reskilling within firms. It outlines five components specific to self-skilling, termed "Self-Skilling Factors," alongside two measurable benefits from reskilling, termed "Reskilling Outcomes." Additionally, there are two elements that bridge the gap between these sets, known as the "Mediators". ESSM® is a modified version of SSM published in my PhD thesis with three moderating elements for the entire phenomenon added to the original model. Each of these twelve components are detailed in the subsequent sections.

Self-Skilling Factors

Learning Agility

Definition: This construct Learning Agility used in ESSM® measures the employee's willingness and ability to learn new competencies to perform under first-time, tough, or different conditions.

Many research studies have drawn connections between lifelong learning competency, particularly in learning agility, to the ability for self-directed learning and problem-solving. Among all the elements that define learning agility, self-directed learning stands out as the most influential. Employees in an organizational setting flourish when the work environment fosters adaptability, allowing them to unlearn old methods and embrace new approaches, even when faced with resistance. An individual's mindset geared towards continuous growth significantly influences both their personal output and the overarching organizational culture. Consequently, many organizations have turned to learning agility as a benchmark for evaluating an employee's potential for long-term contributions. In the ESSM® context, this metric assesses not only an individual's immediate contributions but also their potential to benefit the organization in future roles or capacities.

Job Design

Definition: This construct Job Design used in ESSM® measures the automatability de-risk of tasks and skills associated with the employee's job profile

The design of an employee's job has a direct impact on their performance. Studies have shown that when jobs are designed with relational contracts—requiring interaction with others—it often leads to more expansive roles for employees. Implementing well-thought-out job designs with inherent rewards can replace the need for additional performance metrics to gauge an employee's contributions. Research indicates a positive correlation between job design and employee commitment, suggesting that a well-structured job can enhance an employee's dedication to effectively fulfilling their responsibilities. Job enrichment, through horizontal or vertical expansion, offers opportunities for employees to acquire new skills. Direct interactions with customers, a facet of job crafting, enables employees to gain insights from client experiences, thereby enhancing their value to the organization. The importance of designing jobs that emphasize enrichment, client interactions, intrinsic rewards, teamwork, and a diverse skill set is well recognized in today's professional environment.

Lately, the structure of jobs in organizations is undergoing swift transformations due to rapid automation. This acceleration is leading to a reduced longevity of specific job skills. Skills acquired early in a career are quickly becoming outdated, highlighting the importance of continuous reskilling throughout one's professional life. This constant evolution of skills has also escalated the costs associated with upskilling and retraining employees. Employees who utilize their innate human capabilities, such as critical thinking, creativity, decision-making, and effective communication, offer greater value to their organizations. In contrast, jobs that operate on a set of instructions and do not leverage these unique human attributes are more susceptible to automation. These jobs are often deemed redundant, posing a threat to the employment security of those holding such positions. According to the Job Characteristics Model by Oldman and Hackman, there are five critical dimensions to any job: skill diversity, task identity, task significance, job autonomy, and feedback. All these aspects are being influenced by the evolving nature of today's workplace. Employees whose roles require a broad range of intricate human skills, which cannot be automated through mere instructions, face a reduced risk of job redundancy. Such employees are naturally inclined towards self-directed learning, thanks to the nature of their roles, fostering a culture of lifelong learning.

Technology

Definition: The construct Technology used in ESSM® measures the employee's behavioral intention to use technology for learning

Leveraging technology for educational purposes, or eLearning, has profound advantages not only for companies but also for their employees. Implementing an eLearning model based on organizational needs can lead to reduced expenses while amplifying benefits for both the employee and the company. Providing training on-demand through technology platforms not only streamlines the training process but also boosts employee efficiency.

Such platforms offer adaptable options for employees, resulting in cost reductions, enhanced worker productivity, and superior performance for businesses. It has been observed that the adoption of eLearning plays a pivotal role in an employee's dedication to their organization, leading to heightened production rates and increased motivation levels. The relationship between eLearning utilization by employees and aspects like job efficiency, performance satisfaction, and organizational loyalty often hinges on the synergy between eLearning methodologies and managerial backing. Research indicates that the duration employees invest in tech-based learning has a direct correlation with performance enhancement.

However, an excessive workload can hinder the time devoted to learning, potentially making the benefits of eLearning underutilized. Those employees who adeptly harness technology for skill enhancement typically achieve superior outcomes in their reskilling efforts and can more effectively apply what they have learned to their roles. Such employees tend to offer greater value to their employers, showcasing improved efficiency, higher productivity levels, and maintaining their relevance within their respective industries.

Culture

Definition: The Culture construct used in ESSM® measures the employee's support for self-skilling from the organization's leadership and culture

Organizational culture plays a pivotal role in influencing an employee's inclination toward learning. By instilling a culture of continuous learning, organizations can foster deeper ties with employees, aligning them with long-term strategic objectives. An organization that prioritizes learning from experiences, fosters consistent growth, and creates a conducive environment for learning empowers its workforce. This, in turn, enhances employee commitment and dedication toward achieving company goals.

A strong learning culture boosts both employee satisfaction and performance, which can subsequently elevate the financial health of the organization. By offering a diverse range of learning opportunities, organizations can uplift employee performance and alignment with broader company objectives. Approaching employee development with a focus on equipping them to fulfil organizational goals can amplify their contribution and efficacy. The presence of a robust learning culture is key to optimizing the contributions of employees. In such cultures, leaders and managers play the role of mentors, guiding employees to augment their value to the organization.

When innovation is nurtured within a learning-centric environment, leaders shepherd the process of idea generation while encouraging continuous learning among employees. Recognizing and rewarding self-driven learning endeavours by employees can lead to enhanced outcomes in reskilling, benefiting the organization at large.

Perception

Definition: The Perception construct used in ESSM® measures the employee's perception about self-skilling

Employees are diverse in their approach to workplace learning, and their individual views on the advantages of self-skilling can determine both their learning choices and their overall contributions to the organization. Their interpretation of the company's learning culture can significantly impact the value they provide. If employees do not envision themselves progressing to senior roles, they may only engage in essential training. Organizations that convey the importance of continuous learning for future roles can reshape employee perceptions and foster a self-skilling culture.

Research indicates that workers with less education might be sceptical about training benefiting their career growth, making their approach to training distinct from that of highly educated workers. Factors like perceived training advantages, available support, and potential impacts on job quality can shape their perspectives. Individuals are often driven to pursue continuous learning opportunities due to anticipated personal growth, job satisfaction, and the need to adapt to societal changes. Ultimately, when employees recognize the mutual benefits of self-skilling for both themselves and the organization, they are more likely to engage in upskilling or reskilling, enhancing their value and alignment with the company's objectives.

Mediating Factors

Mediating factors are intervening elements linked to a particular phenomenon whose existence explains the connection between two other related factors. In the ESSM® framework, three such mediating elements influence the relationship between Self-Skilling Factors and Reskilling Outcomes. These are the Employee's Extrinsic Motivation for Self-Skilling, Intrinsic Motivation for Self-Skilling, and the Employee's Professional Identity. Within ESSM®, the Employee's Professional Identity is also viewed as a Reskilling outcome, representing personal advancement for the employee while simultaneously impacting their value to the organization.

Motivation

Self-skilling is the process of independently engaging in learning activities, driven by one's motivation. Drawing from psychology, the theory of motivation provides insights into human actions across various domains. There are two primary types of motivation: intrinsic and extrinsic. Intrinsic motivation is driven by personal enjoyment and inherent satisfaction from an activity, while extrinsic motivation stems from the desire to achieve specific outcomes or rewards. Both these types of motivations collectively determine an individual's intention and actual engagement in an activity. The motivation theory has been explored in relation to self-directed learning.

Extrinsic Motivation

Definition: The construct Extrinsic Motivation used in ESSM® measures the extrinsic factors that drive the employee to self-skilling

Extrinsic motivation relates to external elements such as rewards, penalties, or external consequences stemming from an individual's self-skilling efforts. For example, an employee adept at quick learning and leveraging technology for self-skilling, and who perceives positively the benefits and support for self-skilling, may be motivated by external rewards like job completion satisfaction, high assessment scores, promotions, or other incentives. Though the initiation of self-skilling might be personal, it is the extrinsic motivators that often sustain and guide the effort toward achieving specific goals.

Intrinsic Motivation

Definition: The construct Intrinsic Motivation used in ESSM® measures the intrinsic factors of personality that drive the employee to self-skilling

An individual's personality shapes their values. What one values due to their unique personality fulfils their innate desires, fostering an intrinsic motivation for self-skilling. Furthermore, extrinsic motivation can activate and positively impact intrinsic motivation factors, such as a passion for learning or responsiveness to experiences, among others.

Reskilling Outcomes

Employee Relevance

Definition: The construct Employee Relevance used in ESSM® measures employee's value for the organization in terms of productivity, alignment, and contribution

The need for reskilling is crucial to ensure an employee's continued relevance to an organization. Governments globally recognize the urgency of keeping the workforce updated with evolving skills. With the world's rapid changes, it is essential for people to continuously adapt, learn, and relearn to remain pertinent. Traditionally, the foundational skills imparted in schools and universities were deemed sufficient for a lifelong career, with any additional training provided by employers. However, with increasing complexities in job roles, there is a growing emphasis on continuous education.

The speed at which changes are occurring means that initial education might not sustain an individual throughout their career. Hence, the concept of continuous reskilling becomes imperative. Beyond the individual implications, such as lost wages and mental well-being challenges, there are societal ramifications including reduced productivity, declined tax contributions, and increased healthcare and crime costs. Governments should proactively support reskilling initiatives, mirroring the rapid changes in the workplace. The World Economic Forum had estimated that by 2020, 35% of job skills would shift, and this prediction has now risen to 40% by 2025 due to the pandemic. The skill set required by the labour market is in a constant state of evolution, further emphasized by recent global events.

Employee Professional Identity

*Definition: The construct of Employee Professional Identity used in ESSM®
measures the strength of the employee's professional identity*

The evolution of job roles and the necessity for reskilling deeply influence an employee's sense of professional identity. In the modern work environment, loyalty to both employer and chosen profession is central to this identity challenge. Constructive professional examples can pave the way for shaping this identity.

Key components of professional identity include career ambition, understanding one's work domain, self-confidence, and future goals. Aspects like race, gender, and social class play roles in moulding this identity. Any restructuring in the workforce, especially that which leads to deskilling, can impact an individual's sense of professional identity. Alterations in work-related policies can similarly influence this identity. For those undergoing career changes, redefining one's professional identity typically aligns closer to their previous role. The professional community offers pivotal support, helping maintain a consistent identity amidst change.

Established professionals might need to validate, reframe, and culturally readjust to navigate shifts in their professional logic. The integration and use of Internet and Communication Technologies (ICT) can enhance the identities of professionals, particularly in fields like science. An employee's designated job role, defined by job design, plays a crucial role in crafting their professional identity. Several studies have identified the impact of technology assimilation on professional identity. Moreover, organizational culture significantly shapes the construction of an employee's professional identity.

Understanding and Leveraging ESSM® for the Future of Work

The Employee Self-Skilling Model (ESSM)®) outlines key factors for organizations to optimize reskilling outcomes, both now and in the evolving world of work. Within ESSM®, five pivotal elements are identified that pertain to self-skilling: Employee's Learning Agility, Job Design, Perception about Self-Skilling, Intention to Utilize Technology for Learning, and the support an employee derives from leadership and the organizational culture. Two principal benefits arise from employee reskilling: the enhancement of an employee's professional identity and a boost in their significance to the organization.

All the elements driving self-skilling profoundly impact both the individual's professional identity and their organizational relevance. Motivation acts as a critical bridge between self-skilling and its results. Elements of self-skilling spark and influence extrinsic motivational factors. For instance, a particular job design might create a task-driven necessity, urging the employee to undertake self-learning. The intention to harness technology for learning can also prompt the desire to learn from eLearning resources and experts.

While these extrinsic motivational elements are born from self-skilling factors, they can further stimulate intrinsic motivation, catering to deeper personal needs, such as a genuine passion for learning. External motivators for self-skilling can range from accessing essential information, meeting compliance mandates, succeeding in assessments, and the allure of learning itself. On the other hand, intrinsic motivators include a love for learning, empowerment from expertise, adaptability, proactiveness, and risk-taking tendencies.

ESSM® dispels a common misconception held by many organizational leaders. Instead of fearing the loss of employees with a robust professional identity, ESSM® highlights that nurturing such an identity can indeed boost their value and alignment with organizational objectives.

Moderating Factors

Moderating factors are elements linked to the phenomenon that modify the intensity or direction of the connection between the other related factors. In the ESSM® framework, three such moderating elements influence the relationship between Self-Skilling Factors and Reskilling Outcomes. These are the Employee's Demographic Profile, Career Profile, and Spend Profile. These elements include the factors like employee's age, gender, educational background, work experience, digital dexterity, income level, frequency of job rotations in their career, number of years spent in a particular role, willingness and actual spending of money from own earnings for Self-Skilling. According to ESSM® all these factors significantly modify the reskilling outcomes from self-skilling.

The primary driving force behind self-skilling lies with the individual. Self-skilling plays a crucial role in the broader concept of reskilling. As the work landscape evolves, individuals will need to emphasize self-skilling, fostering learning agility, becoming adept at digital tools, and embracing technological advancements in learning. Achieving a balanced approach to job rotations, with substantial time spent in each role, can solidify an individual's professional identity and relevance.

On the contrary, frequent job switches can diminish both identity and relevance. Merely investing in numerous courses or accumulating certifications without strategic insight isn't the solution during this era of reskilling. Instead, informed decisions regarding higher education and understanding the job market and one's strengths are essential.

While the essence of self-skilling is woven into individual learning processes, it often remains an untapped resource in many organizational training initiatives. The focus predominantly rests on explicit educational aspects, with the subtler, implicit aspects of knowledge transfer, rooted in an individual's work habits and on-the-job experiences, often overlooked. However, by strategically integrating self-skilling, organizations can foster a self-perpetuating environment for ongoing upskilling and reskilling. The Employee Self-skilling Model (ESSM)® , illustrated in Figure 5.2, outlines the interplay between individual and organizational factors influencing self-skilling.

Through ESSM®, businesses can elevate their upskilling and reskilling initiatives, leading to enhanced employee performance and value. The main arena for skill acquisition and implicit learning is the workplace.

While educational institutions prepare individuals for the job market, they primarily cater to explicit learning needs. The true essence of implicit learning and knowledge application thrives in the professional environment. By employing the ESSM® framework, companies can amplify the inherent self-skilling tendencies of their employees, resulting in quicker skill proficiency and potentially reducing reskilling costs, establishing a joint responsibility shared between organizations and their staff.

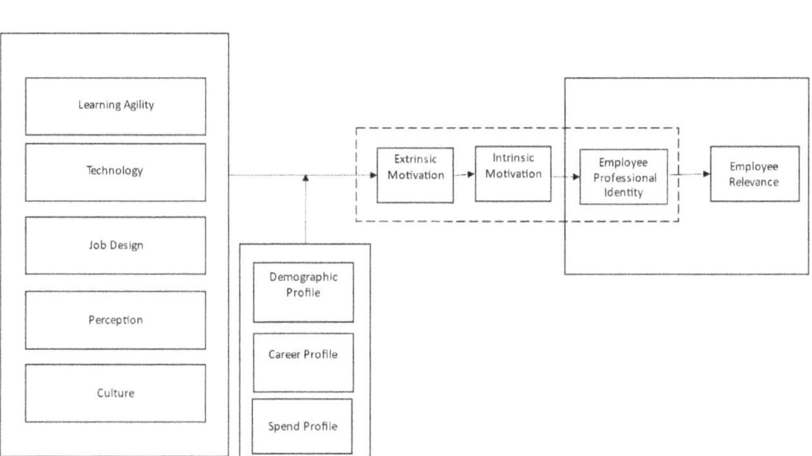

Figure 5.2 *Employee Self Skilling Model (ESSM)®*

"The individual's role is agentic to the success of reskilling journeys. Organizations can leverage individual self-skilling for reskilling employees by using the Employee Self-Skilling Model (ESSM)® that reveals the forces that move this phenomenon."

PART III

Employee Self Skilling, Reskilling, & Future of Work

CHAPTER – 6

Circular Talent Management

During my initial stint in a corporate HR role, I had the chance to work closely with the HR leader of the business. One day, she posed a question about using the term "people" over "resources" in our daily work discussions related to employees. This reflection has lingered with me ever since. While academic management often labels individuals as "human resources" for businesses, I ponder whether they are just resources or, in fact, the very essence of a business. While personally, I resonate more with the latter view, in this chapter, I introduce one of the well-known concepts of resource management, 'Circular Economy', to the most essential resource for any business – the human resource.

The principle of 'Circular Economy' emphasizes on sustainability through sharing, leasing, reusing, repairing, refurbishing, and recycling of resources, and offers an alternative to the traditional linear usage of resources. Applying this to human resources implies minimizing layoffs and instead optimizing the talent pool. This could involve job rotations, engaging people in secondment projects, additional role assignments, targeted training, upskilling, and reskilling when employees demonstrate a heightened potential. I have termed this approach "Circular Talent Management." It is an essential concept for business leaders and HR professionals, especially in these ever-evolving times. As job roles and skill requirements consistently evolve, reskilling becomes the beacon for nurturing adaptability and ensuring continuous contribution of people to an organization.

Much like how the conventional linear economy consumes, produces, and then discards resources, the prevalent trend of mass layoffs in businesses pushes society to perceive individuals as disposable assets. A proactive approach to maximize potential of every employee by reskilling will not only solve for talent crisis of the business but pave the way for sustainable development by preserving the dignity of one of the most precious resources on the planet, that is the "Human Resource".

The primary goal of reskilling people is to ensure they remain engaged, valuable, and consequently, indispensable to the world of work. Six foundational principles of a more holistic human resource approach can empower organizations and nations to implement Circular Talent Management.

Self-directed learning culture – Cultivate an environment where individuals are constantly learning, dedicating time to hone new abilities, and are eager to tackle new challenges. As we navigate the wave of reskilling, promoting a self-learning ethos becomes essential for both individuals and institutions, making it a foundation for the evolving workplace landscape in every corporation and country.

Synergistic Collaboration in the world of work – Champion a work culture where organizations actively share, delegate, and maximize their human resources both internally and externally. The rise of the gig economy, legal moonlighting, sanctioned secondment projects and deputations outside the organization, and contractual work positions signal the direction modern HRM is taking. Such structures not only bolster an individual's employability but also provide organizations with a nimble approach to workforce management.

Combating Career Derailers – Equip individuals with 'Evergreen Skills' to navigate challenging and potentially career-stalling situations. These skills, relevant to the modern age, are indispensable for every individual. I am discussing more about these skills in the next book.

Individual Professional Identity – Advocate for, Educate, and Enable conscious construction of professional identity for individuals. Every reskilling journey would involve individuals to fortify their new professional stature. This is as crucial for enterprises as it is for the individuals, since the more robust an employee's professional image, the more significant is their contribution to the organization's success.

Golden Years in Education – With increasing life expectancies and evolving employment avenues, every nation must gear up to engage the older generation of workforce, those in their post-retirement span of life, often referred as 'Golden Years'. Institutions offering education and training should gear up to facilitate age agnostic learning journeys and instil the importance of self-directed learning skills, upskilling, and reskilling as a lifelong phenomenon.

Leveraging Boundaryless Talent – Implementing Circular Talent Management will require a shift in the mindset of both organizations and individuals to accept the boundarylessness of human talent. This would mean adoption of new employment models, seamless exchange of human resource and effective collaboration between businesses. While this might seem a distant possibility today to most of us reading this, the success of gig platforms is an early positive signal towards such future reality. It resonates so well with an extract I read from Swami Vivekananda's discourse.

> *"Some say that if man did not fight man, he would not progress. I also used to think so, but I find now that every war has thrown back human progress by fifty years instead of hurrying it forwards. The day will come when men will study history from a different light and find that* ***competition is neither the cause nor the effect, simply a thing on the way, not necessary to evolution at all***.*"*

> – *Swami Vivekananda*

If businesses learn to collaborate with the intent to nurture and preserve the human essence, we can discover new avenues for sustained growth both for individuals and organizations in the work world.

If we are to visualise the individual's professional identity as a plant, it is fascinating to understand just how inseparable the "WE", the root, is from the "ME", the shoot. This emerging paradigm in the new era is calling on humanity to collaborate rather than compete.

The six foundational pillars of "Circular Talent Management" discussed above underscore the essence of "Career Self Governance" and "Sustainable Professional Growth" for working individuals. While managing one's career trajectory seems inherently an individual's responsibility, it truly flourishes with the combined efforts of enterprises, governments, educational bodies, and above all, our society.

As businesses add the sustainability dimension to their Balance Score Cards to support the achievement of the United Nations Sustainable Development Goals for the world, environmental sustainability and CSR objectives have started getting focus at scale. There is a pressing need to also integrate goals focused on circular talent strategies—emphasizing reskilling and reallocating roles to reduce workforce redundancy and layoffs. It is through these efforts that we can ensure enduring growth and stability not just for businesses but also for mankind as a whole.

CHAPTER – 7

Traversing the Reskilling Revolution with Self-Skilling

Globally, there is a noticeable rise in employee layoffs, a surge in unemployment rates, and a decline in labour force participation. Yet, amidst this trend of job cuts, there is a concurrent drive to hire for new, especially tech-related, roles that require fresh skills. This presents a contrasting scenario with significant workforce demand in various sectors and the proliferation of educational and skill development solutions.

An individual's competence and performance are no longer the sole determinants of career stability. The looming possibility of unemployment hangs over virtually every working individual. Research indicates that those affected by layoffs generally find new roles within a span of one month to a year. The traditional notion of a single qualification leading to a lifelong career is becoming obsolete.

To navigate the uncertainties of the modern work environment, professionals must continually adapt, either by acquiring diverse skills while on the job or by transitioning into new professions. Continuous reskilling throughout one's career is essential to maintain relevance in the evolving job market. For companies to bridge immediate talent shortages and ensure long-term sustainable development, investing in workforce reskilling is crucial.

The Employee Self Skilling Model (ESSM)®, discussed in chapter five, asserts that nearly 70% of an organization's reskilling outcomes hinge on certain individual-specific factors. Formulating strategies around these factors can amplify the benefits of reskilling programs. This chapter delves into the implications for the primary entities involved, providing insights to successfully navigate the ongoing reskilling wave.

Readiness of Education & Training Solution Providers for Lifelong Learning

Global educational institutions are adapting to meet the reskilling demands of the industry 4.0. Traditional academic centres are launching a variety of new courses, degrees, and diploma programs tailored for the reskilling of established professionals. Admission procedures are becoming less age-restrictive, welcoming mid-career professionals from diverse age brackets.

Additionally, these institutions are not just providing educational services but also assisting these professionals in transitioning careers through placement programs. Enhanced collaboration between industries and academia, both for skill training and collaborative research to address industry challenges, is further strengthening these modern educational endeavours.

Circular Talent Goals in Balance Score Card of organizations

The prevalence of reskilling initiatives is growing within many organizations. Top-tier management should consider integrating "circular talent goals" into their performance metrics to minimize layoffs, rejuvenate human resources through reskilling, and redeploy staff into novel roles. Business and HR leaders should craft strategies to keep their current employees by pinpointing roles prone to obsolescence and preparing these workers for alternative positions.

Moreover, companies should consider offering diverse career pathways, such as flexible workforce models, entrepreneurial partnerships, and legal moonlighting, allowing them to benefit from employees' skills while offering more flexible, long-term employment commitments in the VUCA business environment.

Adoption of Heutagogy Principles in Formal Education

A purely vocational approach to education may lead to a restricted perspective, grooming students for roles that may soon become obsolete. Formal Higher Education has been observed to greatly influence the refinement of human skills, thus amplifying individuals' reskilling outcomes. The NEP 2020's strategy for vocational education in India hints at a promising trajectory, as it integrates vocational studies with opportunities for further education.

Heutagogy, or self-driven learning, champions an instructional paradigm that prioritizes student autonomy and capability development. This approach gears learners towards a lifelong learning ethos, preparing them for the multifaceted challenges of the modern workforce. Unlike traditional structured learning, heutagogy embodies a more spontaneous, informal method, mirroring how most individuals acquire knowledge outside educational institutions.

Here, educators transition from primary knowledge providers to supportive mentors. Introduced by Hase and Kenyon in 2000, heutagogy sets itself apart from pedagogy (teacher-led learning) and andragogy (self-guided learning). In a heutagogical setting, students are not just task executors; they actively identify uncertainties and delve into complex aspects of their subjects. Educators assist by offering context and crafting avenues for comprehensive exploration.

This learning style demands higher student maturity, minimal teacher interference, and enables students to transition from mere absorbers of knowledge to analytical thinkers and integrators. Students are not only engaged in deep contemplation of the topic but also introspect on the learning methodologies.

This cultivates learners who perpetually challenge their preconceptions and glean insights into their learning processes. For educational institutions aiming to foster self-skilling tendencies in their pupils, strategies like learner-driven learning contracts, adaptive curriculum, collaborative learning engagements, and fluid assessments, as opposed to rigid ones, could be instrumental.

Focus on Developing Learning Agility of Employees

Is Learning Agility an innate trait or can it be nurtured? A considerable body of research and experimental data suggests that Learning Agility can indeed be cultivated. Many modern organizations are now integrating Learning Agility into their competency models and have deployed tools to assess and enhance this competency among their workforce. That being said, the education sector also has a pivotal role in shaping future talents.

It is vital that educational outcomes encompass the development of learning agility and the intrinsic drive for self-skilling, as highlighted in the ESSM®. Educational bodies should consistently evaluate and foster these abilities in students using established Self-Directed Learning (SDL) readiness metrics throughout their educational journey.

In corporate environments, departments like HR, L&D, and managerial teams should re-evaluate and reshape learning and performance strategies to foster learning agility and instil a culture of perpetual learning. Efforts should be made to cultivate a positive attitude towards self-skilling by recognizing and promoting its benefits. Advanced AI-driven technologies can be harnessed to offer personalized learning experiences, encouraging self-driven skilling among employees.

Interestingly, there is empirical evidence suggesting that seasoned employees often achieve superior reskilling results. HR teams should actively counteract biases, ensuring that reskilling opportunities aren't skewed by age or gender-based misconceptions. In the current landscape, many organizations have Diversity, Equity, and Inclusion (DEI) advocates. Such champions should keep a vigilant eye on reskilling outcomes, especially for female employees, ensuring equity in opportunities and outcomes.

Substantial modifications in job design are necessary. HR and Organizational Development (OD) experts need to ensure that employees are consistently engaged in tasks demanding cognitive, social, and emotional human intelligence. By leveraging the Employee Self-skilling Model (ESSM)®, organizations can reimagine workplace learning, setting the foundation for a robust culture of autonomous skilling and continuous learning.

Like its predecessors, the current Industrial Revolution 4.0 promises enhanced societal well-being, elevated living standards, enriched job roles, and an overall improvement in our quality of life. While it offers businesses heightened productivity, efficiency, and profitability, it also ushers in the immense task of widespread workforce reskilling.

If we neglect the education and training of upcoming generations, the repercussions could be stark – from widening income disparities and heightened unemployment to increased reliance on governmental support and amplified migratory movements. This evolution is steering us towards roles that prioritize creativity and meaning over mere task execution.

The legitimacy theory posits that organizations gain more credibility when they prioritize societal sustainability, aligning with stakeholder expectations. Embracing the principles of Industry 5.0 not only addresses stakeholder concerns but also bolsters business competitiveness. Therefore, it is crucial for both organizations and nations to strategically facilitate the seamless transition of the current and future workforce into the evolving job landscape, ensuring sustainable progress.

In today's evolving work landscape, continuous upskilling and reskilling are becoming imperative for every individual. As industries undergo transformation and technology progresses, the need for consistent learning will only intensify. While technological advancements and the education system have responded by offering training and educational solutions, a significant challenge persists: a growing segment of the workforce will essentially be newcomers in their roles. This encompasses both existing employees adapting to new skills and fresh graduates entering the workspace.

A majority of this workforce, while newly educated, might not possess the expertise to excel immediately with their recently acquired skills. Achieving proficiency and mastery over these skills demands substantial practice and hands-on experience. This shift underscores the importance of experiential learning in the reskilling journey. Traditional on-the-job training methods may not be sufficient anymore. The Employee Self-Skilling Model (ESSM)® offers HR and L&D professionals a targeted approach, emphasizing certain key elements to strategically cultivate a sustainable environment for continuous learning, upskilling, and reskilling within their establishments.

Our world is in the midst of a profound shift, with virtually every facet undergoing rejuvenation. Advances in AI pinpoint several crucial skills that humans will need to stay relevant both economically and socially. These include:

- Digital dexterity – the ability to collaborate and operate seamlessly with AI.
- Rapid self-learning capabilities to adapt to and integrate emerging technologies.
- Non-algorithmic creativity that leverages personal knowledge and experience for problem-solving.
- Social proficiency for effective interactions with peers and clients.
- The ability to push the boundaries of these technologies further.
- An understanding of sustainable living, emphasizing lifelong learning and fostering a better world for subsequent generations.

Central to acquiring these pivotal skills is the concept of self-skilling. This domain, poised to thrive, intersects with multiple disciplines including psychology, cognitive science, social science, management, technology, and education. Surprisingly, despite its evident significance, the research arena has largely overlooked self-skilling.

This book not only offers an exhaustive exploration of the topic but also introduces the innovative Employee Self-Skilling Model (ESSM)®. An evidence-backed framework, ESSM® is specifically tailored for in-organization employee reskilling. By harnessing insights from ESSM®, talent strategies can be optimized, accentuating the vital contribution of individuals in their reskilling endeavours.

"A proactive approach to maximize the potential of every employee by reskilling will not only solve the talent crisis but pave the way for sustainable development by preserving the dignity of one of the most precious resources on the planet – the human resource."

References

Adepoju, O. (2022). Reskilling for Construction 4.0. In Re-skilling Human Resources for Construction 4.0 (pp. 197–219). Springer, Cham. 10.1007/978-3-030-85973-2-9

Adepoju, O. O., & Aigbavboa, C. O. (2021). Assessing knowledge and skills gap for construction 4.0 in a developing economy. Journal of Public Affairs, 21(3), e2264. 10.1002/pa.2264

Agrawal, S., De Smet, A., Lacroix, S., & Reich, A. (2020). To emerge stronger from the COVID-19 crisis, companies should start reskilling their workforces now. McKinsey Insights.

Ajzen, I. (1991). The theory of planned behavior. Organizational Behavior and Human Decision Processes, 50(2), 179–211.

Akther, J. (2020). Influence of UNESCO in the Development of Lifelong Learning. Open Journal of Social Sciences, 8(3), 103–112.

Al Mamun, M. A., Lawrie, G., & Wright, T. (2020). Instructional design of scaffolded online learning modules for self-directed and inquiry-based learning environments. Computers & Education, 144, 103695. 10.1016/j.compedu.2019.103695

Al-Ababneh, M. (2020). Linking ontology, epistemology, and research methodology. Science & Philosophy, 8(1), 75–91.

Alabdulkareem, A., Frank, M. R., Sun, L., AlShebli, B., Hidalgo, C., & Rahwan, I. (2018). Unpacking the polarization of workplace skills. Science Advances, 4(7), eaao6030.

Alagaraja, M., & Herd, A. M. (2022). Understanding Multi-level Learning in Organizations: A Comparison of Lean and the Learning Organization. Performance Improvement Quarterly, 34(4), 521–546. 10.1002/piq.21364

Ali, F., & Tan, S. C. (2022). Emotions and lifelong learning: synergies between neuroscience research and transformative learning theory. International Journal of Lifelong Education, 1–15.

Ali, N., & Zia-ur-Rehman, M. (2014). Impact of job design on employee performance, mediating role of job satisfaction: A study of FMCG's sector in Pakistan. International Journal of Business and Management, 9(2), 70.

Al-Na'ama, M. R., Alkafajei, A. M. B., & Joseph, G. (1980). Profile of the medical student and his outlook on medical education—the Basrah experience. Medical education, 14(6), 401–408. 10.1111/j.1365–2923.1980.tb02391.x

Anangisye, W. A., & Barrett, A. M. (2005). Professional identity and misconduct: Perspectives of Tanzanian teachers. Southern African Review of Education with Education with Production, 11(1), 5–22.

Annuar, N., & Shaari, R. (2014). The antecedents toward self-directed learning among distance learner in Malaysian public universities. Proceeding of the Global Summit on Education GSE, 4–5.

Apple, M. W. (1981). Curricular form and the logic of technical control. Economic and Industrial Democracy, 2(3), 293–319. 10.1177/0143831X8123002

Artis, A. B., & Harris, E. G. (2007). Self-directed learning and sales force performance: An integrated framework. Journal of Personal Selling & Sales Management, 27(1), 9–24.

Asogwa, B. E., Ezeani, C. N., & Asogwa, M. N. (2021). Status of electronic records management (e-RM) in African university libraries: experience from Nigerian universities. Library Management. 10.1108/LM-04–2021–0036

Atack, L. (2003). Becoming a web-based learner: registered nurses' experiences. Journal of advanced nursing, 44(3), 289–297. 10.1046/j.1365–2648.2003.02804.x

Atack, L., & Rankin, J. (2002). A descriptive study of registered nurses' experiences with web-based learning. Journal of Advanced Nursing, 40(4), 457–465. 10.1046/j.1365–2648.2002.02394.x

Ausburn, L. J. (2002). The freedom versus focus dilemma in a customized self-directed learning environment: A comparison of the perceptions of adult and younger students. Community College Journal of Research and Practice, 26(3), 225–235. 10.1080/106689202317245428

Baber, H. (2021). Modelling the acceptance of e-learning during the pandemic of COVID-19-A study of South Korea. The International Journal of Management Education, 19(2), 100503. 10.1016/j.ijme.2021.100503

Backes-Gellner, U., & Veen, S. (2013). Positive effects of ageing and age diversity in innovative companies–large-scale empirical evidence on company productivity. Human Resource Management Journal, 23(3), 279–295.

Bailey, L. (2015). Reskilled and 'Running Ahead': Teachers in an international school talk about their work. Journal of Research in International Education, 14(1), 3–15.

Bakkenes, I., Vermunt, J. D., & Wubbels, T. (2010). Teacher learning in the context of educational innovation: Learning activities and learning outcomes of experienced teachers. Learning and instruction, 20(6), 533–548. 10.1016/j. learninstruc.2009.09.001

Bandura, A. (1988). Organisational applications of social cognitive theory. Australian Journal of Management, 13(2), 275–302.

Bandura, A. (2005). The evolution of social cognitive theory. Great Minds in Management, 9–35.

Bandura, A., & Schunk, D. H. (1981). Cultivating competence, self-efficacy, and intrinsic interest through proximal self-motivation. Journal of personality and social psychology, 41(3), 586. 10.1037/0022–3514.41.3.586

Barjesteh, H., Movafaghardestani, E., & Modaberi, A. (2020). COVID-19's impact on digitalization of education: incorporating visual vocabulary learning application to foster vocabulary knowledge. Asian Education and Development Studies. 10.1108/AEDS-05–2020–0111

Barros, R. (2012). From lifelong education to lifelong learning. Discussion of some effects of today's neoliberal policies. European Journal for Research on the Education and Learning of Adults, 3(2), 119–134.

Bartholomew, S. R., Reeve, E. M., Veon, R., Goodridge, W., Lee, V. R., & Nadelson, L. (2017). Relationships between access to mobile devices, student self-directed learning, and achievement. Journal of Technology Education, 29(1), 2.

Bartlett, J. E., Kotrlik, J. W., & Higgins, C. C. (n.d.). Organizational Research: Determining Appropriate Sample Size in Survey Research. 8.

Basak, E., & Calisir, F. (2014). Uses and gratifications of LinkedIn: An exploratory study. Proceedings of the World Congress on Engineering, 2, 1–4.

Baskett, H. K. (1993). Workplace Factors Which Enhance Self-Directed Learning. A Report of a Project on Self-Directed Learning in the Workplace.

Beard, V. (1994). Popular culture and professional identity: Accountants in the movies.Accounting, Organizations and Society, 19(3), 303–318.

Becker, E. A., & Gibson, C. C. (1998). Fishbein and Ajzen's theory of reasoned action: Accurate prediction of behavioral intentions for enrolling in distance education courses. Adult Education Quarterly, 49(1), 43–55.

Bedford, C. L. (2011). The role of learning agility in workplace performance and career advancement.

Beer, M. (2002). Building organizational fitness in the 21st century. Division of Research, Harvard Business School.

Bennett, E. E., & McWhorter, R. R. (2021). Virtual HRD's role in crisis and the post Covid-19 professional lifeworld: Accelerating skills for digital transformation. Advances in Developing Human Resources, 23(1), 5–25. 10.1177/1523422320973288

Bennett, R. (2010). What makes a marketer? Development of 'marketing professional identity' among marketing graduates during early career experiences. Journal of Marketing Management, 27(1–2), 8–27.

Bentler, P. M., & Wu, E. J. (2005). EQS 6.1 for Windows. Structural equations program manual. Encino, CA: Multivariate Software

Benzidia, S., Makaoui, N., & Bentahar, O. (2021). The impact of big data analytics and artificial intelligence on green supply chain process integration and hospital environmental performance. Technological forecasting and social change, 165, 120557. 10.1016/j.techfore.2020.120557

Berg, S. A., & Chyung, S. Y. Y. (2008). Factors that influence informal learning in the workplace. Journal of workplace learning. 10.1108/13665620810871097

Bessen, J. (2014). Employers aren't just whining–the "skills gap" is real. Harvard Business Review, 25.

Biemans, H., Nieuwenhuis, L., Poell, R., Mulder, M., & Wesselink, R. (2004). Competence-based VET in the Netherlands: Background and pitfalls. Journal of vocational education and training, 56(4), 523–538. 10.1080/13636820400200268

Billett, S. (2015). Work, discretion, and learning: processes of life learning and development at work. International Journal of Training Research, 13(3), 214–230. 10.1080/14480220.2015.1093308

Billett, S. (2021). Mediating worklife learning and the digitalisation of work. British Journal of Educational Technology, 52(4), 1580–1593. 10.1111/bjet.13115

Billionniere, E., & Meyer, L. (2021, October). Transforming Education: Upskilling for a Cloudy Tomorrow. In Proceedings of the 22st Annual Conference on Information Technology Education (pp. 91–96). 10.1145/3450329.3476863

Bissell, D. (2021). Encountering automation: Redefining bodies through stories of technological change. Environment and Planning D: Society and Space, 39(2), 366-384. 10.1177/0263775820963128

Blomstrom, D. (2020). Humans versus Machines: Who Will Still Have a Job in 50 Years? The AI Book: The Artificial Intelligence Handbook for Investors, Entrepreneurs and FinTech Visionaries, 262–264.

Blumberg, P., & Michael, J. A. (1992). Development of self-directed learning behaviors in a partially teacher-directed problem-based learning curriculum. Teaching and Learning in Medicine: An International Journal, 4(1), 3–8. 10.1080/10401339209539526

Blynova, O., Lappo, V., Kalenchuk, V., Agarkov, O., Shramko, I., Lymarenko, L., & Popovych, I. (2020). CORPORATE CULTURE OF A HIGHER EDUCATION INSTITUTION AS A FACTOR IN FORMING STUDENTS' PROFESSIONAL IDENTITY. Revista Inclusiones, 481–496.

Bodkyn, C., & Stevens, F. (2015). Self-directed learning, intrinsic motivation and student performance. The Caribbean Teaching Scholar, 5(2).

Bok, H. G., Teunissen, P. W., Favier, R. P., Rietbroek, N. J., Theyse, L. F., Brommer, H., ... & Jaarsma, D. A. (2013). Programmatic assessment of competency-based workplace learning: when theory meets practice. BMC medical education, 13(1), 1–9. 10.1186/1472-6920-13-123

Bolhuis, S. (2003). Towards process-oriented teaching for self-directed lifelong learning: a multidimensional perspective. Learning and instruction, 13(3), 327–347. 10.1016/S0959-4752(02)00008-7

Boticki, I., Baksa, J., Seow, P., & Looi, C. K. (2015). Usage of a mobile social learning platform with virtual badges in a primary school. Computers & Education, 86, 120–136. 10.1016/j.compedu.2015.02.015

Boud, D., & Middleton, H. (2003). Learning from others at work: communities of practice and informal learning. Journal of workplace learning. 10.1108/13665620310483895

Bouri, I., & Reponen, S. (2021, November). Elements of AI: Busting AI Myths on a Global Scale. In 21st Koli Calling International Conference on Computing Education Research (pp. 1–2). 10.1145/3488042.3490513

Boyatzis, R. E. (1994). Stimulating self-directed learning through the managerial assessment and development course. Journal of Management Education, 18(3), 304–323. 10.1177/105256299401800303

Boyer, S. L., Edmondson, D. R., Artis, A. B., & Fleming, D. (2014). Self-directed learning: A tool for lifelong learning. Journal of Marketing Education, 36(1), 20–32. 10.1177/0273475313494010

Brown, J., Gosling, T., Sethi, B., Sheppard, B., Stubbings, C., Sviokla, J., Williams, J., Zarubina, D., & Fisher, L. (2017). Workforce of the future: The competing forces shaping 2030. London: PWC.

Brown, K. G. (2005). A field study of employee e-learning activity and outcomes. Human Resource Development Quarterly, 16(4), 465–480.

Bruch, H., & Ghoshal, S. (2002). Beware the busy manager. Harvard Business Review, 80(2), 62–69.

Brugger, F., & Gehrke, C. (2018). Skilling and deskilling: Technological change in classical economic theory and its empirical evidence. Theory and Society, 47(5), 663–689.

Brussevich, M., Dabla-Norris, M. E., & Khalid, S. (2020). Who will bear the brunt of lockdown policies? Evidence from tele-workability measures across countries. International Monetary Fund.

Brydges, R., & Butler, D. (2012). A reflective analysis of medical education research on self-regulation in learning and practice. Medical education, 46(1), 71–79. 10.1111/j.1365–2923.2011.04100.x

Bryman, A. (1984). The debate about quantitative and qualitative research: A question of method or epistemology? British Journal of Sociology, 75–92.

Burdett, J. O. (1991). To coach, or not to coach–that is the question! Part 2. Industrial and Commercial Training.

Burrus, J., Jackson, T., Xi, N., & Steinberg, J. (2013). Identifying the most important 21st century workforce competencies: An analysis of the Occupational Information Network (O* NET). ETS Research Report Series, 2013(2), i–55.

Busby, R. D. (2019). Upskilling, Reskilling and Learning Agility.

Byrne, B. M. (2001). Structural equation modeling with AMOS, EQS, and LISREL: Comparative approaches to testing for the factorial validity of a measuring instrument. International Journal of Testing, 1(1)

Cameron, L. M. (2021). English Language Teacher Associations and the Exclusivity of Professional Development. Research on Teaching and Learning English in Under-Resourced Contexts. 10.4324/9781003057284–8

Campion, M. A., Cheraskin, L., & Stevens, M. J. (1994). Career-related antecedents and outcomes of job rotation. Academy of Management Journal, 37(6), 1518–1542.

Candra, S., Cahyono, H., Wibowo, R. A., & Sutopo, T. (2020). Acceptance of the use of social media: Case of linkedin in Indonesian netizen. International Journal of Scientific and Technology Research, 9(1), 1451–1461.

Canrinus, E. T., Helms-Lorenz, M., Beijaard, D., Buitink, J., & Hofman, A. (2012). Self-efficacy, job satisfaction, motivation, and commitment: Exploring the relationships between indicators of teachers' professional identity. European Journal of Psychology of Education, 27(1), 115–132.

Casad, S. (2012). Implications of job rotation literature for performance improvement practitioners. Performance Improvement Quarterly, 25(2), 27–41.

Chakma, S., & Chaijinda, N. (2020). Importance of reskilling and upskilling the workforce. วารสาร สห ศาสตร์ ศรีปทุม ชลบุรี Interdisciplinary Sripatum Chonburi Journal (ISCJ), 6(2), 23–31.

Chan, M. K., Dickson, G., Keegan, D. A., Busari, J. O., Matlow, A., & Van Aerde, J. (2021). A tale of two frameworks: charting a path to lifelong learning for physician leaders through CanMEDS and LEADS. Leadership in Health Services.

Cheng, E. W., & Hampson, I. (2008). Transfer of training: A review and new insights. International journal of management reviews, 10(4), 327–341. 10.1111/j.1468–2370.2007.00230.x

Cheng, E. W., Li, H., Love, P., & Irani, Z. (2004). A learning culture for strategic partnering in construction. Construction Innovation.

Cheng, Y. M. (2012). Effects of quality antecedents on e-learning acceptance. Internet Research. 10.1108/10662241211235699

Cheng, Y.-M. (2011). Antecedents and consequences of e-learning acceptance. Information Systems Journal, 21(3), 269–299.

Chigbu, B. I., & Nekhwevha, F. H. (2021). The future of work and uncertain labour alternatives as we live through the industrial age of possible singularity: Evidence from South Africa. Technology in Society, 67, 101715. 10.1016/j.techsoc.2021.101715

Cho, E., & Lee, J. (n.d.). Korean Journal of Military Arts and Science.

Chue, S., Säljö, R., Lee, Y. J., & Pang, E. L. W. (2022). Spills and thrills: internship challenges for learning in epistemic spaces. Journal of Education and Work, 1–14. 10.1080/13639080.2021.2018410

Ciccone, A., & Papaioannou, E. (2009). Human capital, the structure of production, and growth. The Review of Economics and Statistics, 91(1), 66–82.

Clardy, A. (2000). Learning on their own: Vocationally oriented self-directed learning projects. Human Resource Development Quarterly, 11(2), 105–125.

Clochard, A., & Westerman, G. (2020). Understanding the incumbent worker's decision to train: The challenges facing less-educated workers. MIT Industrial Performance Center. https://jwel. mit. edu/sites/mit-jwel ....

Cónego, L., Pinto, R., & Goncalves, G. (2021, November). Education 4.0 and the Smart Manufacturing Paradigm: A Conceptual Gateway for Learning Factories. In Working Conference on Virtual Enterprises (pp. 721–728). Springer, Cham. 10.1007/978-3-030-85969-5-68

Confessore, S. J., & Kops, W. J. (1998). Self-directed learning and the learning organization: Examining the connection between the individual and the learning environment. Human resource development quarterly, 9(4), 365–375.

Cooper, D. R., & Schindler, P. S. (2006). Marketing research. New York: McGraw-Hill/Irwin.

Correia, A.-P., Hickey, S., Lepicki, T., & Willis, A. (2021). Meeting Online Learners Where They Are: E-Learning during a time of pandemic. ELearn, 2021(8).

Costello, C. Y. (2005). Professional identity crisis: Race, class, gender, and success at professional schools. Vanderbilt University Press.

Crespo, P. A. M., Fernández, O. M., & Pedrero-García, E. (2022). Negative stereotypes towards older people: A study with teachers in initial training. Revista Electrónica Educare, 26(1), 1–20.

Csordás, A. (2020). Diversifying effect of digital competence. AGRIS On-Line Papers in Economics and Informatics, 12(665–2020–1220), 3–13.

Dai, K., Nespereira, C. G., Vilas, A. F., & Redondo, R. P. D. (2015). Scraping and clustering techniques for the characterization of LinkedIn profiles. ArXiv Preprint ArXiv: 1505.00989.

Darrah, C. (1992). Workplace skills in context. Human Organization, 51(3), 264–273.

Darwin, A. (2000). Critical reflections on mentoring in work settings. Adult education quarterly, 50(3), 197–211. 10.1177/07417130022087008

Daud, K. A. M., Khidzir, N. Z., Parasuraman, B., Bhattacharyya, E., Savita, K. S., Rao, P. V., … & Aris, R. (2021, July). Employability skills: What do employers need?. In AIP Conference Proceedings (Vol. 2347, No. 1, p. 020032). AIP Publishing LLC. 10.1063/5.0052149

de Meuse, K. P., Dai, G., Hallenbeck, G. S., & Tang, K. Y. (2008). Using learning agility to identify high potentials around the world. Korn/Ferry Institute, 1–22.

Deci, E. L. (1975). Intrinsic motivation. New York: Plenum Press.

Deci, E. L., & Ryan, R. M. (1981). Curiosity and Self-Directed Learning: The Role of Motivation in Education.

Deepa, V., Sujatha, R., & Baber, H. (2021). Ageing and Learning Agility–Mediating role of learning perception and Moderating role of technology leverage. International Journal of Lifelong Education, 40(5–6), 514–531. 10.1080/02601370.2021.1991501

Deepa V., Shukla B, Sujatha R., Mohan J (2022). Leveraging Self-skilling–A Tool for Reskilling Employees within Organizations, Amity University PhD Thesis

Deepa, V., Sujatha, R., & Mohan, J. (2022). Unsung voices of technology in school education-findings using the constructivist grounded theory approach. Smart Learning Environments, 9(1), 1–25. 10.1186/s40561–021–00182–7

DeKeyser, R., VanPatten, B., & Williams, J. (2007). Skill acquisition theory. Theories in Second Language Acquisition: An Introduction, 97113.

Delen, E., Liew, J., & Willson, V. (2014). Effects of interactivity and instructional scaffolding on learning: Self-regulation in online video-based environments. Computers & Education, 78, 312–320. 10.1016/j.compedu.2014.06.018

Deuze, M., Martin, C. B., & Allen, C. (2007). The professional identity of gameworkers. Convergence, 13(4), 335–353.

DeVellis, R. F., Lewis, M. A., & Sterba, K. R. (2003). Interpersonal emotional processes in adjustment to chronic illness. Social psychological foundations of health and illness, 256–287.

Dhanraj, D., & Parumasur, S. B. (2014). Perceptions of the impact of job rotation on employees, productivity, the organization and on job security. Corporate Ownership & Control, 11(4), 682–691.

Dickinson, L. (1979). Self-instruction in commonly-taught languages. System, 7(3), 181–186. 10.1016/0346–251X(79)90001–0

Diethert, A. P., Weisweiler, S., Frey, D., & Kerschreiter, R. (2015). Training motivation of employees in academia: Developing and testing a model based on the theory of reasoned action. In Motivationsforschung im Weiterbildung-skontext (pp. 29–50). Springer.

Digwo, U., Oderinde, D., & Brown-Huston, M. (2010). 'Leveraging e-learning in organizations: Challenges, benefits and models for adoption'. UK Academy for Information Systems Conference Proceedings.

Dixon, M. A. (2021). Finding Joy in the Journey: Sustaining a Meaningful Career in Sport Management. Journal of Sport Management, 1(aop), 1–8.

Dorenbosch, L., Engen, M. L. van, & Verhagen, M. (2005). On-the-job innovation: The impact of job design and human resource management through production ownership. Creativity and Innovation Management, 14(2), 129–141.

Dornan, T., Boshuizen, H., King, N., & Scherpbier, A. (2007). Experience-based learning: a model linking the processes and outcomes of medical students' workplace learning. Medical education, 41(1), 84–91. 10.1111/j.1365–2929.2006.02652.x

Douglass, C., & Morris, S. R. (2014). Student perspectives on self-directed learning. Journal of the Scholarship of Teaching and Learning, 13–25.

Dries, N., Vantilborgh, T., & Pepermans, R. (2012). The role of learning agility and career variety in the identification and development of high potential employees. Personnel Review.

du Toit Brits, C. (2018). Towards a transformative and holistic continuing self-directed learning theory. South African Journal of Higher Education, 32(4), 51–65.

Du, X., Lundberg, A., Ayari, M. A., Naji, K. K., & Hawari, A. (2022). Examining engineering students' perceptions of learner agency enactment in problem-and project-based learning using Q methodology. Journal of Engineering Education, 111(1), 111–136. 10.1002/jee.20430

Dymock, D., & McCarthy, C. (2006). Towards a learning organization? Employee perceptions. The Learning Organization.

Dynan, L., Cate, T., & Rhee, K. (2008). The impact of learning structure on students' readiness for self-directed learning. Journal of education for business, 84(2), 96–100. 10.3200/JOEB.84.2.96–100

Economy, W. E. F. C. for the N., & Group (BCG), S. B. C. (2019). Towards a reskilling revolution: Industry-led action for the future of work.

Edirisooriya, W. A. (2014). Impact of rewards on employee performance: With special reference to ElectriCo. Proceedings of the 3rd International Conference on Management and Economics, 26(1), 311–318.

Egan, T. M., Yang, B., & Bartlett, K. R. (2004). The effects of organizational learning culture and job satisfaction on motivation to transfer learning and turnover intention. Human Resource Development Quarterly, 15(3), 279–301.

Eichbaum, Q. G. (2014). Thinking about thinking and emotion: The metacognitive approach to the medical humanities that integrates the humanities with the basic and clinical sciences. The Permanente Journal, 18(4), 64.

Ellis, H. C., Ottaway, S. A., Varner, L. J., Becker, A. S., & Moore, B. A. (1997). Emotion, motivation, and text comprehension: the detection of contradictions in pas – sages. Journal of Experimental Psychology: General, 126(2).

Ellström, P. E. (2010). Practice-based innovation: a learning perspective. Journal of Workplace learning. 10.1108/13665621011012834

Engeström, Y. (2004). New forms of learning in co-configuration work. Journal of Workplace learning. 10.1108/13665620410521477

Engeström, Y., & Kerosuo, H. (2007). From workplace learning to inter-organizational learning and back: the contribution of activity theory. Journal of workplace learning. 10.1108/13665620710777084

Escobari, M., Seyal, I., & Meaney, M. (2019). Realism about Reskilling. Brookings Institution, November, 7.

Estrin, L., Foreman, J. T., & Garcia, S. (2003). Overcoming barriers to technology adoption in small manufacturing enterprises (SMEs). Carnegie-Mellon Univ Pittsburgh PA Software Engineering Inst.

Eva, K. W., & Regehr, G. (2011). Exploring the divergence between self-assessment and self-monitoring. Advances in health sciences education, 16(3), 311–329. 10.1007/s10459–010–9263–2

Ezeanolue, E. T., & Ezeanyim, E. E. (2020). Employee Participation In Decision Making And Organizational Productivity In Manufacturing Firms In South-East, Nigeria.

Fadel, C. (2008). 21st Century Skills: How can you prepare students for the new Global Economy. Diunduh Dari: Https://Www. Oecd. Org/Site/Educe–ri21st/40756908. Pdf.

Fagan, M. H., Neill, S., Wooldridge, B. R. (2008). Exploring the intention to use computers: An empirical investigation of the role of intrinsic motivation, extrinsic motivation, and perceived ease of use. The Journal of Computer Information Systems, 48(3).

Fagermoen, M. S. (1997). Professional identity: Values embedded in meaningful nursing practice. Journal of Advanced Nursing, 25(3), 434–441.

Fake, H., & Dabbagh, N. (2021, October). The Personalized Learning Interaction Framework: Expert Perspectives on How to Apply Dimensions of Personalized Learning to Workforce Training and Development Programs. In Ninth International Conference on Technological Ecosystems for Enhancing Multiculturality (TEEM'21) (pp. 501–509). 10.1145/3486011.3486503

Fearon, J. D. (1999). What is identity (as we now use the word). Unpublished Manuscript, Stanford University, Stanford, Calif.

Fenlon, M. J., & Fitzgerald, B. K. (2019). Reskilling–A solution for the digital skills gap. PricewaterhouseCoopers, Place of publication not identified.

Fenwick, T. (2014). Knowledge circulations in inter-para/professional practice: a sociomaterial enquiry. Journal of Vocational Education & Training, 66(3), 264–280. 10.1080/13636820.2014.917695

Fichman, R. G., & Kemerer, C. F. (1997). The assimilation of software process innovations: An organizational learning perspective. Management Science, 43(10), 1345–1363.

Field, A. (2009). Discovering statistics using SPSS. Sage publications

Fischer, G. (2001). Lifelong learning and its support with new media. International Encyclopedia of Social and Behavioral Sciences, 13(41), 1–7.

Fisher, M., King, J., & Tague, G. (2001). Development of a self-directed learning readiness scale for nursing education. Nurse education today, 21(7), 516–525. 10.1054/nedt.2001.0589

Flanagan, B., Nestel, D., & Joseph, M. (2004). Making patient safety the focus: crisis resource management in the undergraduate curriculum. Medical education, 38(1), 56–66. 10.1111/j.1365–2923.2004.01701.xFluid Intelligence—An overview | ScienceDirect Topics. (n.d.). Retrieved April 16, 2022, from https://www.sciencedirect.com/topics/psychology/fluid-intelligence

Forum, W. E. (2017). Accelerating workforce reskilling for the fourth industrial revolution: An agenda for leaders to shape the future of education, gender, and work.

Forum, W. E. (2020). The future of jobs report 2020.

Fottler, M. D. (2005). Job analysis and job design. Human Resources in Healthcare, 133–161.

Frambach, J. M., Driessen, E. W., Chan, L. C., & van der Vleuten, C. P. (2012). Rethinking the globalisation of problem-based learning: how culture challenges self-directed learning. Medical education, 46(8), 738–747. 10.1111/j.1365–2923.2012.04290.x

GA, S. P., MJ, M. R., & Vieites, R. (2021). Competitive Debate as Innovation in Gamification and Training for Adult Learners: A Conceptual Analysis. Frontiers in psychology, 12, 666871–666871.

Gabrielle, D. (2003). The effects of technology-mediated instructional strategies on motivation, performance, and self-directed learning. EdMedia+ Innovate Learning, 2568–2575.

Gallagher, S. A. (1997). Problem-based learning: Where did it come from, what does it do, and where is it going?. Journal for the Education of the Gifted, 20(4), 332-362. 10.1177/016235329702000402

Galperin, R. V. (2017). Mass-production of professional services and pseudo-professional identity in tax preparation work. Academy of Management Discoveries, 3(2), 208–229.

Garavan, T. N., & McGuire, D. (2001). Competencies and workplace learning: some reflections on the rhetoric and the reality. Journal of Workplace learning. 10.1108/13665620110391097

García Vaquero, M., Sánchez-Bayón, A., & Lominchar, J. (2021). European Green Deal and Recovery Plan: Green Jobs, Skills, and Wellbeing Economics in Spain. Energies, 14(14), 4145. 10.3390/en14144145

Garland, R. (1991). The mid-point on a rating scale: Is it desirable. Marketing Bulletin, 2(1)

Garrison, D. R. (1992). Critical thinking and self-directed learning in adult education: An analysis of responsibility and control issues. Adult education quarterly, 42(3), 136–148. 10.1177/074171369204200302

Garrison, D. R. (1997). Self-directed learning: Toward a comprehensive model. Adult Education Quarterly, 48(1), 18–33.

George, J. M., & Brief, A. P. (1996). Motivational agendas in the workplace: The effects of feelings on focus of attention and work motivation. Elsevier Science/ JAI Press

Gerber, R., Lankshear, C., Larsson, S., & Svensson, L. (1995). Self-directed learning in a work context. Education+ Training.

Gestrelius, K. (1979). Lifelong Education--a New Challenge. European Journal of Science Education, 1(3), 277–292. 10.1080/0140528790010303

Ghosh, S., & Muduli, A. (2021). Learning agility, culture, and outcome: An empirical study. International Journal of Indian Culture and Business Management, 23(1), 95–110.

Giancola, F. L. (2011). Examining the job itself as a source of employee motivation. Compensation & Benefits Review, 43(1), 23–29.

Gibbons, M., Bailey, A., Comeau, P., Schmuck, J., Seymour, S., & Wallace, D. (1980). Toward a theory of self-directed learning: A study of experts without formal training. Journal of Humanistic Psychology, 20(2), 41–56.

Gokcearslan, S. (2017). Perspectives of students on acceptance of Tablets and self-directed learning with technology. Contemporary Educational Technology, 8(1), 40–55.

Görmüş, A. (2019). Future of work with the industry 4.0. International Congress on Social Sciences (INCSOS 2019) Proceeding Book, 1(32), 317–323.

Goyal, S. (2012). E-Learning: Future of education. Journal of Education and Learning, 6(2), 239–242.

Graen, G., Novak, M. A., & Sommerkamp, P. (1982). The effects of leader—member exchange and job design on productivity and satisfaction: Testing a dual attachment model. Organizational Behavior and Human Performance, 30(1), 109–131.

Granitz, N. A., Koernig, S. K., & Harich, K. R. (2009). Now it's personal: Antecedents and outcomes of rapport between business faculty and their students. Journal of Marketing Education, 31(1), 52–65.

Griffin, R. W., & McMahan, G. C. (2013). Motivation through job design. In Organizational behavior (pp. 33–54). Routledge.

Grow, G. O. (1991). Teaching learners to be self-directed. Adult education quarterly, 41(3), 125–149. 10.1177/0001848191041003001

Grunau, P. (2016). The impact of overeducated and undereducated workers on establishment-level productivity: First evidence for Germany. International Journal of Manpower.

Guerrero, M., Heaton, S., & Urbano, D. (2021). Building universities' intrapreneurial capabilities in the digital era: The role and impacts of Massive Open Online Courses (MOOCs). Technovation, 99, 102139. 10.1016/j.technovation.2020.102139

Guglielmino, L. M. (1977). Development of the self-directed learning readiness scale. University of Georgia.

Gürbüz, O. C. A. K., & Karakuyu, A. (2021). Investigation of The Relationship Between Lifelong Learning and Epistemological Beliefs of Associate Degree Students'. Participatory Educational Research, 9(2), 136–149.

Gureckis, T. M., & Markant, D. B. (2012). Self-directed learning: A cognitive and computational perspective. Perspectives on Psychological Science, 7(5), 464–481. 10.1177/1745691612454304

Gurubatham, M. R. (2014). Enlivening fluid intelligence in blended active learning within the cognitive literacy value chain framework. Procedia-Social and Behavioral Sciences, 123, 238–248.

Guthrie, J. T. (2004). Teaching for literacy engagement. Journal of literacy research, 36(1), 1–30. 10.1207/s15548430jlr3601_2

Guthrie, J. T., Wigfield, A., & VonSecker, C. (2000). Effects of integrated instruction on motivation and strategy use in reading. Journal of educational psychology, 92(2), 331. 10.1037/0022–0663.92.2.331

Hair, J. F., Black, W. C., Babin, B. J., Anderson, R. E., & Tatham, R. L. (2006). Multivariate data analysis 6th Edition. Pearson Prentice Hall. New Jersey. humans: Critique and reformulation. Journal of Abnormal Psychology, 87, 49–74.

Hair, J. F., Tatham, R. L., Anderson, R. E., & Black, W. (2006). Multivariate data analysis (6th ed.). London: Pearson Education (US).

Hallam, J. (2012). Nursing the image: Media, culture, and professional identity. Routledge.

Hamdan, K. M., Al-Bashaireh, A. M., Zahran, Z., Al-Daghestani, A., Samira, A. H., & Shaheen, A. M. (2021). University students' interaction, Internet self-efficacy, self-regulation, and satisfaction with online education during pandemic crises of COVID-19 (SARS-CoV-2). International Journal of Educational Management. 10.1108/IJEM-11–2020–0513

Hammer, A., & Karmakar, S. (2021). Automation, AI, and the Future of Work in India. Employee Relations: The International Journal.

Hammersley-Fletcher, L., & Qualter, A. (2009). Chasing improved pupil performance: The impact of policy change on school educators' perceptions of their professional identity, the case of further change in English schools. British Educational Research Journal, 36(6), 903–917.

Hao, Y. (2016). Exploring undergraduates' perspectives and flipped learning readiness in their flipped classrooms. Computers in Human Behavior, 59, 82–92. 10.1016/j.chb.2016.01.032

Harding, T. S., Vanasupa, L., Savage, R. N., & Stolk, J. D. (2007). Work-in-progress-Self-directed learning and motivation in a project-based learning environment. 2007 37th Annual Frontiers In Education Conference-Global Engineering: Knowledge Without Borders, Opportunities Without Passports, F2G-3.

Harris, B. (2009). 'Extra appendage'or integrated service? School counsellors' reflections on their professional identity in an era of education reform. Counselling and Psychotherapy Research, 9(3), 174–181.

Harrison, R. (1978). How to design and conduct self-directed learning experiences. Group & Organization Studies, 3(2), 149–167.10.1177/105960117800300203

Hashim, J. (2008). Competencies acquisition through self-directed learning among Malaysian managers. Journal of Workplace Learning.

Hatane, S. E. (2015). Employee satisfaction and performance as intervening variables of learning organization on financial performance. Procedia-Social and Behavioral Sciences, 211, 619–628.

Hellstrom, J. (2010) The innovative use of mobile applications in East Africa, SIDA Review 2010: 12, Swedish International Development Cooperation Agency, Stockholm.

Hernandez, P. R., Bloodhart, B., Barnes, R. T., Adams, A. S., Clinton, S. M., Pollack, I., Godfrey, E., Burt, M., & Fischer, E. V. (2017). Promoting professional identity, motivation, and persistence: Benefits of an informal mentoring program for female undergraduate students. Plos One, 12(11), e0187531.

Hibbert, S., Winklhofer, H., & Temerak, M. S. (2012). Customers as resource integrators: toward a model of customer learning. Journal of Service Research, 15(3), 247–261. 10.1177/1094670512442805

Hicks, D. (2013). Technology and Professional Identity of Librarians: The Making of the Cybrarian: The Making of the Cybrarian. IGI Global.

Hill, L. A. (2004). New manager development for the 21st century. Academy of Management Perspectives, 18(3), 121–126.

Hindi, A. M., Willis, S. C., & Schafheutle, E. I. (2022). Using communities of practice as a lens for exploring experiential pharmacy learning in general practice: Are communities of practice the way forward in changing the training culture in pharmacy?. BMC medical education, 22(1), 1–10. 10.1186/s12909–021–03079–8

Hinkin, T. R. (1995). A review of scale development practices in the study of organizations. Journal of Management, 21(5), 967–988.

Hinkin, T. R. (1998). A brief tutorial on the development of measures for use in survey questionnaires. Organizational research methods, 1(1)

Ho, L. A. (2008). What affects organizational performance? The linking of learning and knowledge management. Industrial Management & Data Systems.

Ho, L. A. (2011). Meditation, learning, organizational innovation, and performance. Industrial Management & Data Systems.

Ho, L.-A. (2009). The antecedents of e-learning outcome: An examination of system quality, technology readiness, and learning behavior. Adolescence, 44(175).

Hodkinson*, H., & Hodkinson, P. (2005). Improving schoolteachers' workplace learning. Research papers in education, 20(2), 109–131. 10.1080/026715 20500077921

Hoeve, Y. ten, Jansen, G., & Roodbol, P. (2014). The nursing profession: Public image, self-concept, and professional identity. A discussion paper. Journal of Advanced Nursing, 70(2), 295–309.

Holzer, H. J. (1990). The determinants of employee productivity and earnings. Industrial Relations: A Journal of Economy and Society, 29(3), 403–422.

Hooper, D., Coughlan, J., & Mullen, M. R. (2008). Structural Equation Modeling: Guidelines for Determining Model Fit. The Electronic Journal of Business Research Methods, 6(1).

Hopwood, N., Dahlberg, J., Blomberg, M., & Abrandt Dahlgren, M. (2022). Double stimulation in healthcare emergencies: fostering expansive, collective tool use through simulation-based continuing professional education. Pedagogy, Culture & Society, 30(1), 71–87. 10.1080/14681366.2020.1805496

Horn, I. S., & Little, J. W. (2010). Attending to problems of practice: Routines and resources for professional learning in teachers' workplace interactions. American educational research journal, 47(1), 181–217. 10.3102/0002831209345158

Howard, D. (2017). Learning agility in education: Analysis of pre-service teacher's learning agility and teaching performance. Tarleton State University.

Hsu, T. C. (2017). Learning English with augmented reality: Do learning styles matter?. Computers & Education, 106, 137–149. 10.1016/j.compedu.2016.12.007

Hu, L. T., & Bentler, P. M. (1999). Cutoff criteria for fit indices in covariance structure analysis: Conventional criteria versus new alternatives. Structural Equation Modeling, 6.

Huang, A. Y., Fisher, T., Ding, H., & Guo, Z. (2021). A network analysis of cross-occupational skill transferability for the hospitality industry. International Journal of Contemporary Hospitality Management. 10.1108/IJCHM-01–2021–0073

Huang, Y.-M. (2021). Innovative Technologies and Learning: 4th International Conference, ICITL 2021, Virtual Event, November 29–December 1, 2021, Proceedings. Springer Nature.

Hung, M. L., Chou, C., Chen, C. H., & Own, Z. Y. (2010). Learner readiness for online learning: Scale development and student perceptions. Computers & Education, 55(3), 1080–1090. 10.1016/j.compedu.2010.05.004

Hung, W. (2011). Theory to reality: A few issues in implementing problem-based learning. Educational Technology Research and Development, 59(4), 529–552. 10.1007/s11423–011–9198–1

Hutasuhut, I. J., Adruce, S. A. Z., & Usop, H. (2019). Antecedent Factors of Self-Directed Learning in the Workplace: A Case Study in a Private Organization in Indonesia. Journal of Cognitive Sciences and Human Development, 5(2), 41–52.

Illeris, K. (2005). Low-skilled workers learn at the workplace. Lifelong Learning in Europe, 3, 172.

Illeris, K. (2006). Lifelong learning and the low-skilled. International journal of lifelong education, 25(1), 15–28. 10.1080/02601370500309451

Ilter, B. G. (2009). Effect of technology on motivation in EFL classrooms. Turkish Online Journal of Distance Education, 10(4), 136–158.

Irby, D. M. (1995). Teaching and learning in ambulatory care settings: a thematic review of the literature. Academic medicine, 70(10), 898–931. 10.1097/00001888-199510000-00014

Isacsson, A., & Gretzel, U. (2011). Facebook as an edutainment medium to engage students in sustainability and tourism. Journal of Hospitality and Tourism Technology.

Jacobs, R. L., & Park, Y. (2009). A proposed conceptual framework of workplace learning: Implications for theory development and research in human resource development. Human resource development review, 8(2), 133–150. 10.1177/1534484309334269

Jagannathan, S. (Ed.). (2021). Reimagining Digital Learning for Sustainable Development: How Upskilling, Data Analytics, and Educational Technologies Close the Skills Gap. Routledge. 10.4324/9781003089698

Jam, N. A. M., & Puteh, S. Exploring the Teaching and Learning Indicators towards Education 4.0 in MTUN, Malaysia. 10.18178/ijiet.2022.12.2.1602

Janacsek, K., Fiser, J., & Nemeth, D. (2012). The best time to acquire new skills: Age-related differences in implicit sequence learning across the human lifespan. Developmental Science, 15(4), 496–505.

Jang, K., Kim, J., & Chang, W. (2021). Deskilling and reskilling of political refugees in the Republic of Korea: an actor-network analysis. International Journal of Lifelong Education, 40(3), 281–294. 10.1080/02601370.2021.1956613

Jena, P. K. (2020). Impact of pandemic COVID-19 on education in India. International Journal of Current Research (IJCR), 12.

Jeon, J. (2022). Exploring a self-directed interactive app for informal EFL learning: A self-determination theory perspective. Education and Information Technologies, 1–21.

Jiusto, S., & DiBiasio, D. (2006). Experiential learning environments: Do they prepare our students to be self-directed, life-long learners?. Journal of Engineering Education, 95(3), 195–204. 10.1002/j.2168-9830.2006.tb00892.x

Johari, J. (n.d.). Nurturing Winners in our Early Learners: Re-Defining. 20M35, 77.

Johns, G. (2010). Some unintended consequences of job design. Journal of Organizational Behavior, 31(2/3), 361–369.

Kampelmann, S., & Rycx, F. (2012). The impact of educational mismatch on firm productivity: Evidence from linked panel data. Economics of Education Review, 31(6), 918–931.

Kamphuis, C., Barsom, E., Schijven, M., & Christoph, N. (2014). Augmented reality in medical education?. Perspectives on medical education, 3(4), 300–311. 10.1007/s40037-013-0107-7

Kaplan, H. E., & Hassler, D. M. (1978). The play of education: Volunteer teachers in Experimental University Classes. Alternative Higher Education, 3(1), 51–61. 10.1007/BF01080651

Kar, S., Kar, A. K., & Gupta, M. P. (2021). Understanding the S-Curve of Ambidextrous Behavior in Learning Emerging Digital Technologies. IEEE Engineering Management Review. 10.1109/EMR.2021.3107344

Karacay, G. (2018). Talent development for Industry 4.0. In Industry 4.0: Managing the digital transformation (pp. 123–136). Springer.

Karakas, F., & Manisaligil, A. (2012). Reorienting self-directed learning for the creative digital era. European Journal of Training and Development.

Karatepe, O. M., Uludag, O., Menevis, I., Hadzimehmedagic, L., & Baddar, L. (2006). The effects of selected individual characteristics on frontline employee performance and job satisfaction. Tourism Management, 27(4), 547–560.

Karimi, S. (2016). Do learners' characteristics matter? An exploration of mobile-learning adoption in self-directed learning. Computers in Human Behavior, 63, 769–776.

Keenan, Q. (n.d.). Adult Learning in the Workplace.

Kehoe, R. R., & Wright, P. M. (2013). The impact of high-performance human resource practices on employees' attitudes and behaviors. Journal of Management, 39(2), 366–391.

Kek, M., & Huijser, H. (2011). Exploring the combined relationships of student and teacher factors on learning approaches and self-directed learning readiness at a Malaysian university. Studies in Higher Education, 36(2), 185–208.

Kemp, K., Baxa, D., & Cortes, C. (2022). Exploration of a Collaborative Self-Directed Learning Model in Medical Education. Medical science educator, 1–13. 10.1007/s40670-021-01493-7

Khatib Zanjani, N., Ajam, A. A., & Badnava, S. (2017). Determining the relationship between self-directed learning readiness and acceptance of e-learning and academic achievement of students. Iran Journal of Nursing, 30(106), 11–22.

Khobai, H., & Moyo, C. (2021). Trade openness and industry performance in SADC countries: is the manufacturing sector different?. International Economics and Economic Policy, 18(1), 105–126. 10.1007/s10368–020–00476–0

Kline, R. B. (2011). Convergence of structural equation modeling and multilevel modeling

Kokkodis, M., & Ipeirotis, P. G. (2021). Demand-aware career path recommendations: A reinforcement learning approach. Management Science, 67(7), 4362–4383. 10.1287/mnsc.2020.3727

Kop, R. (2011). The challenges to connectivist learning on open online networks: Learning experiences during a massive open online course. International Review of Research in Open and Distributed Learning, 12(3), 19–38. 10.19173/ irrodl. v12i3.882

Kothari, C. R. (2004). Research methodology: Methods and techniques. New Age International.

Kraak, A. (1987). Uneven capitalist development: A case study of deskilling and reskilling in South Africa's metal industry. Social Dynamics, 13(2), 14–31. 10.1080/02533958708458427

Kramer, D., & Close, R. C. (2004). The revolution in eLearning. Retrieved January, 9, 2009.

Krishnaswamy, K. N., Sivakumar, A. L., & Mathirajan, M. (2006). Management Research Methodology: Integration of Methods and Techniques. Pearson Education India

Kuznia, K. D., & Ellis, P. F. (2014). Corporate elearning impact on employees. Global Journal of Business Research, 8(4), 1–16.

Kwakman, K. (2003). Professional learning throughout the career. International Journal of Human Resources Development and Management, 3(2), 180–190. 10.1504/ IJHRDM.2003.002419

Kyndt, E., Dochy, F., & Nijs, H. (2009). Learning conditions for non-formal and informal workplace learning. Journal of Workplace Learning. 10.1108/13665620910966785

Kyratsis, Y., Atun, R., Phillips, N., Tracey, P., & George, G. (2017). Health systems in transition: Professional identity work in the context of shifting institutional logics. Academy of Management Journal, 60(2), 610–641.

Labonté, C., & Smith, V. R. (2022). Learning through technology in middle school classrooms: Students' perceptions of their self-directed and collaborative learning with and without technology. Education and Information Technologies, 1–16. 10.1007/s10639–021–10885–6

Lai, C. (2013). A framework for developing self-directed technology use for language learning. Language Learning & Technology, 17(2), 100–122.

Lai, C., & Jin, T. (2021). Teacher professional identity and the nature of technology integration. Computers & Education, 175, 104314.

Lai, Y., Saab, N., & Admiraal, W. (2022). University students' use of mobile technology in self-directed language learning: Using the integrative model of behavior prediction. Computers & Education, 179, 104413. 10.1016/j.compedu.2021.104413

Lalitha, T. B., & Sreeja, P. S. (2020). Personalised Self-Directed Learning Recommendation System. Procedia Computer Science, 171, 583–592.

Lallemand, T., & Rycx, F. (2009). Are older workers harmful for firm productivity? De Economist, 157(3), 273–292.

Lamb, R., & Davidson, E. (2005). Information and communication technology challenges to scientific professional identity. The Information Society, 21(1), 1–24.

Lankau, M. J., & Scandura, T. A. (2002). An investigation of personal learning in mentoring relationships: Content, antecedents, and consequences. Academy of Management Journal, 45(4), 779–790.

Lassk, F. G., Ingram, T. N., Kraus, F., & Mascio, R. D. (2012). The future of sales training: Challenges and related research questions. Journal of Personal Selling & Sales Management, 32(1), 141–154.

Lee, J., & Song, J. H. (2021). Developing a measurement of employee learning agility. European Journal of Training and Development.

Leejoeiwara, B. (2013). Modeling adoption intention of online education in Thailand using the extended decomposed theory of planned behavior (DTPB) with self-directed learning. AU Journal of Management, 11(2), 13–26.

Legbeti, O. G. (2021). Employee turnover intentions among bank employees in South Western Nigeria. Nigerian Journal of Social Psychology, 4(1).

Lehtonen, E. E., Nokelainen, P., Rintala, H., & Puhakka, I. (2021). Thriving or surviving at work: how workplace learning opportunities and subjective career success are connected with job satisfaction and turnover intention?. Journal of Workplace Learning. 10.1108/JWL-12–2020–0184

Lemmetty, S., & Collin, K. (2020). Self-directed learning as a practice of workplace learning: Interpretative repertoires of self-directed learning in ICT work. Vocations and Learning, 13(1), 47–70. 10.1007/s12186–019–09228-x

Leong, H., Shaun, A. J., & Singh, M. N. (2016). Enhancing students self-directed learning and motivation. The 12th International CDIO Conference, 739.

Levett-Jones, T. L. (2005). Self-directed learning: Implications and limitations for undergraduate nursing education. Nurse Education Today, 25(5), 363–368. 10.1016/j.nedt.2005.03.003

Li, F., Lu, H., Hou, M., Cui, K., & Darbandi, M. (2021). Customer satisfaction with bank services: The role of cloud services, security, e-learning, and service quality. Technology in Society, 64, 101487. 10.1016/j.techsoc.2020.101487

Lim, H.-W. (2011). Concept maps of Korean EFL student teachers' autobiographical reflections on their professional identity formation. Teaching and Teacher Education, 27(6), 969–981.

Linde, C. (2001). Narrative and social tacit knowledge. Journal of knowledge management. 10.1108/13673270110393202

Little, T. D., Chang, R., Gorrall, B. K., Waggenspack, L., Fukuda, E., Allen, P. J., & Noam, G. G. (2020). The retrospective pretest–posttest design redux: On its validity as an alternative to traditional pretest–posttest measurement. International Journal of Behavioral Development, 44(2), 175–183. 10.1177/0165025419877973

Litzelman, D. K., Stratos, G. A., Marriott, D. J., & Skeff, K. M. (1998). Factorial validation of a widely disseminated educational framework for evaluating clinical teachers. Academic Medicine: Journal of the Association of American Medical Colleges, 73(6), 688–695. 10.1097/00001888–199806000–00016

Liu, K., & Chen, J. M. (2022, January). The mindset, lifelong learning, and gerotranscendence of elderly women in Taiwan: An exploratory study. In Women's Studies International Forum (Vol. 90, p. 102552). Pergamon.

Liu, S. H.-J., & Lan, Y.-J. (2016). Social constructivist approach to web-based EFL learning: Collaboration, motivation, and perception on the use of Google Docs. Journal of Educational Technology & Society, 19(1), 171–186.

Lohman, M. C. (2006). Factors influencing teachers' engagement in informal learning activities. Journal of workplace learning. 10.1108/13665620610654577 Long, H. B. (1989). Theoretical oundations for Self-Directed Learning.

Loyens, S. M., Magda, J., & Rikers, R. M. (2008). Self-directed learning in problem-based learning and its relationships with self-regulated learning. Educational psychology review, 20(4), 411–427. 10.1007/s10648–008–9082–7

Lu, C.-H. (2008). Understanding Self-directed Blended Learner's Usage Behavior of E-learning System [PhD Thesis]. dissertation]. China–Taiwan: National Sun Yat-Sen University.

Luhamya, A. N., Bakkabulindi, F. E., & Muyinda, P. B. (2017). USING THE THEORY OF PLANNED BEHAVIOUR TO EXPLAIN THE INTEGRATION OF ICT IN TEACHING AND LEARNING BY EDUCATORS IN PUBLIC TEACHER TRAINING COLLEGES IN TANZANIA. International Journal of Computing & ICT Research, 11(2).

Lund, S., Madgavkar, A., Manyika, J., Smit, S., Ellingrud, K., Meaney, M., & Robinson, O. (2021). The future of work after COVID-19. McKinsey Global Institute, 18.

Machin, M. A., & Fogarty, G. J. (2004). Assessing the antecedents of transfer intentions in a training context. International Journal of Training and Development, 8(3), 222–236.

Magadlela, D. (2016). Can You Teach a Lion to Roar?: Selected African Skills Development and Capacity Building Perspectives; Breaking Down Old Paradigms and Creating New Opportunities. Institute of Innovation Research, Hitotsubashi University.

Magazine, A. I. (2019). Addressing India's reskilling challenge.

Malkawi, E., Bawaneh, A. K., & Bawa'aneh, M. S. (2020). Campus off, education on: UAEU Students' satisfaction and attitudes towards e-learning and virtual classes during COVID-19 pandemic. Contemporary Educational Technology, 13(1), ep283. 10.30935/cedtech/8708

Malmberg, B., Lindh, T., & Halvarsson, M. (2008). Productivity consequences of workforce aging: Stagnation or Horndal effect? Population and Development Review, 34, 238–256.

Maloney, J., Resnick, M., Rusk, N., Silverman, B., & Eastmond, E. (2010). The scratch programming language and environment. ACM Transactions on Computing Education (TOCE), 10(4), 1–15. 10.1145/1868358.1868363

Mann, K. V. (2011). Theoretical perspectives in medical education: past experience and future possibilities. Medical education, 45(1), 60–68. 10.1111/j.1365-2923.2010.03757.x

Manuti, A., Pastore, S., Scardigno, A. F., Giancaspro, M. L., & Morciano, D. (2015). Formal and informal learning in the workplace: A research review. International journal of training and development, 19(1), 1–17. 10.1111/ijtd.12044

Marra, R. M., Hacker, D. J., & Plumb, C. (2022). Metacognition and the development of self-directed learning in a problem-based engineering curriculum. Journal of Engineering Education, 111(1), 137–161. 10.1002/jee.20437

Marsh, E. (2021). Understanding the effect of digital literacy on employees' digital workplace continuance intentions and individual performance. In Research Anthology on Digital Transformation, Organizational Change, and the Impact of Remote Work (pp. 1638–1659). IGI Global.

Maruca, A. T., Dion, K., Zucker, D., & Kozuch, T. (2021). Significance of self-care management as persons prepare to reintegrate into the community. Journal of Forensic Nursing, 17(2), 107–114. 10.1097/JFN.0000000000000316

Mashelkar, R. A. (2018). Exponential technology, industry 4.0 and future of jobs in India. Review of Market Integration, 10(2), 138–157.

Mason, R. (1988). Computer conferencing: a contribution to self-directed learning. British Journal of Educational Technology, 19(1), 28–41. 10.1111/j.1467-8535.1988.tb00249.x

Masriah, I. (2021). The Influence of Motivation and Work Experience on Employee Productivity. PINISI Discretion Review, 1(1), 331–338.

Matcha, W., Gašević, D., & Pardo, A. (2019). A systematic review of empirical studies on learning analytics dashboards: A self-regulated learning perspective. IEEE Transactions on Learning Technologies, 13(2), 226–245.

Mathis, R. L., Jackson, J. H., & Valentine, S. R. (2015). Human resource management: Essential perspectives. Cengage Learning.

Mattarelli, E., & Tagliaventi, M. R. (2015). How offshore professionals' job dissatisfaction can promote further offshoring: Organizational outcomes of job crafting. Journal of Management Studies, 52(5), 585–620.

Mcadam, R., & Leonard, D. (1999). The contribution of learning organization principles to large-scale business process re-engineering. Knowledge and Process Management, 6(3), 176–183.

McGaghie, W. C., & Menges, R. J. (1975). Assessing self-directed learning. Teaching of Psychology, 2(2), 56–59.10.1207/s15328023top0202_2

Mezirow, J. (1981). A critical theory of adult learning and education. Adult education, 32(1), 3–24. 10.1177/074171368103200101

Milkær, L. R. (2021). The great re-skilling: Understandings of generation, tradition, and nostalgia in everyday-life climate activism. In Climate Change Temporalities (pp. 32–48). Routledge.

Miller, C. (2016). Expectations create outcomes: Growth mindsets in organizations. UNC Executive Development, 1–15.

Mitchinson, A., Gerard, N. M., Roloff, K. S., & Burke, W. W. (2012). Learning agility: Spanning the rigor–relevance divide. Industrial and Organizational Psychology, 5(3), 287–290.

Modimogale, L. L. K., Kroeze, J. H., & Staden, C. J. V. (2021, November). Amending Dynamic Capability Theory for Information Systems Research on the Reskilling of Coal Miners in an AI-Driven Era. In International Conference on Innovative Technologies and Learning (pp. 10–21). Springer, Cham. 10.1007/978-3-030-91540-7_2

Moghaddam, Y., Kwan, S., Freund, L., & Russell, M. G. (2021, July). A Proposed Roadmap to Close the Gap Between Undergraduate Education and STEM Employment Across Industry Sectors. In International Conference on Applied Human Factors and Ergonomics (pp. 363–373). Springer, Cham. 10.1007/978-3-030-80840-2_42

Moon, H., & Hong, S. (2022). The multiple mediating effects of Korean workers' perception of the fourth industrial revolution, career attitudes and future learning intent. European Journal of Training and Development.

Mukherjee, D. V., & Sujatha, R. (2020). "Identity in a Gig Economy", Does Learning Agility Matter?

Mukkerla, L. (2020). Reskillng Indian Workforce: The Need of the Hour. Gavesana Journal of Management, 13(1), 1–6.

Murphy, K. (2012). The social pillar of sustainable development: A literature review and framework for policy analysis. Sustainability: Science, Practice and Policy, 8(1), 15–29.

Musawir, M., Wardi, Y., & Rasyid, R. (2019). The effect of job rotation, compensation and organizational citizenship behaviour on employees' performance of PT Pegadaian (Persero). 2nd Padang International Conference on Education, Economics, Business and Accounting (PICEEBA-2 2018), 741–753.

Naicker, A. S., RehabMed, M., Devi, V., Kailaivasan, P., Saria, B., Yuliawiratman, M.,... & Med, M. M. S. R. (2021). Alternate careers for medical graduates and house officers in Malaysia. Med J Malaysia, 76(2), 183.

Naidoo, J. (2012). Seven steps to innovation success. Management Today, 30(8), 38–42.

Naji, K. K., Du, X., Tarlochan, F., Ebead, U., Hasan, M. A., & Al-Ali, A. K. (2020). Engineering Students' Readiness to Transition to Emergency Online Learning in Response to COVID-19: Case of Qatar. EURASIA Journal of Mathematics, Science and Technology Education, 16(10). 10.29333/EJMSTE/8474

Napathorn, C. (2021). The development of green skills across firms in the institutional context of Thailand. Asia-Pacific Journal of Business Administration. 10.1108/ APJBA-10-2020-0370

Narot, P., & Kiettikunwong, N. (2021). The Trends and Challenges in Education for the Elderly in the Asia-Pacific Region. In Education for the Elderly in the Asia Pacific (pp. 251–268). Springer, Singapore. 10.1007/978–981–16–3326–3_15

Nenniger, P. (1999). On the role of motivation in self-directed learning: The "two-shells-model of motivated self-directed learning" as a structural explanatory concept. European Journal of Psychology of Education, 14(1), 71–86.

Nenty, H. J. (2009). Writing a quantitative research thesis. International Journal of Educational Sciences, 1(1), 19–32.

Nesbit, P. L. (2012). The role of self-reflection, emotional management of feedback, and self-regulation processes in self-directed leadership development. Human Resource Development Review, 11(2), 203–226.

Newton, B., Hurstfield, J., Miller, L., & Bates, P. (2005). Practical tips and guidance on training a mixed-age workforce. Age Partnership Group: Sheffield. OECD (2006) Live Longer, Work Longer. OECD: Paris.

Ngenzi, J. L., Scott, R. E., & Mars, M. (2021). Information and communication technology to enhance continuing professional development (CPD) and continuing medical education (CME) for Rwanda: a scoping review of reviews. BMC Medical Education, 21(1), 1–8.

Nhleko, Y., & Van der Westhuizen, T. (2021, September). Curriculum Alignment: The Perspectives of University Students on the Impact of Industry 4.0 on Entrepreneurship Education Within Higher Education. In European Conference on Innovation and Entrepreneurship (pp. 642-XXX). Academic Conferences International Limited. 10.34190/EIE.21.247

Nikitas, A., Vitel, A. E., & Cotet, C. (2021). Autonomous vehicles and employment: An urban futures revolution or catastrophe?. Cities, 114, 103203. 10.1016/j.cities.2021.103203

Noe, R. A., & Wilk, S. L. (1993). Investigation of the factors that influence employees'participation in development activities. Journal of Applied Psychology, 78(2), 291.

Noe, R. A., Wilk, S. L., Mullen, E. J., & Wanek, J. E. (1997). Employee development: Issues in construct definition and investigation of antecedents. Improving Training Effectiveness in Work Organizations, 153–189.

Norman, G. T., & Schmidt, H. G. (1992). The psychological basis of problem-based learning: A review of the evidence. Academic medicine, 67(9), 557–565. 10.1097/00001888–199209000–00002

Norusis, M. J. (1993). SPSS for Windows: Base system user's guide. USA: SPSS Inc.

Nunnally, J. C. (1978). Psychometric Theory (2nd ed.). New York: McGraw-Hill Inc. Nunnally, J. C., & Bernstein, I. II. (1994) Psychometric theory (3rd ed.). New York, NY: McGraw-Hill, Inc.

Oladele, K. O., Lisoyi, E. O., & Abe, I. I. (2021). Reskilling and Upskilling to Develop Global Relevance in the Fourth Industrial Revolution. In Future of Work, Work-Family Satisfaction, and Employee Well-Being in the Fourth Industrial Revolution (pp. 246–258). IGI Global.

Olivares-Aguila, J., ElMaraghy, W., & ElMaraghy, H. (2021). Human Capital Transformation for Successful Smart Manufacturing. In Towards Sustainable Customization: Bridging Smart Products and Manufacturing Systems (pp. 871–878). Springer, Cham. 10.1007/978-3-030-90700-6-99 Oliver, P. (2013). Writing your thesis. Sage.

Olson, M. H. (2015). Introduction to theories of learning. Psychology Press.

Ordahl, L. E. (1911). Consciousness in relation to learning. The American Journal of Psychology, 22(2), 158–213.

Örtenblad, A. (2004). The learning organization: towards an integrated model. The learning organization. 10.1108/09696470410521592

O'Sullivan, P. S., & Irby, D. M. (2011). Reframing research on faculty development. Academic Medicine, 86(4), 421–428. 10.1097/ACM.0b013e31820dc058

Pandey, N., & Pal, A. (2020). Impact of digital surge during Covid-19 pandemic: A viewpoint on research and practice. International Journal of Information Management, 55, 102171.

Paredes, D., & Fleming-Muñoz, D. (2021). Automation and robotics in mining: Jobs, income, and inequality implications. The Extractive Industries and Society, 8(1), 189–193. 10.1016/j.exis.2021.01.004

Pati, S. P., & Kakani, R. K. (2022). Explaining High Performance Among Indian Administrative Service (IAS) Officers: A Job Demands-Resources Perspective. Review of Public Personnel Administration, 0734371X211062481. 10.1177/0734371X211062481

Payne, S. S., Rundquist, P., Harper, W. V., & Gahimer, J. (2013). Self-directed learning readiness and self-determination for selected rehabilitation professional students: The impact of clinical education. International Journal of Self-Directed Learning, 10(1), 35.

Pedersen, C. S. (2018). The UN sustainable development goals (SDGs) are a great gift to business! Procedia Cirp, 69, 21–24.

Pfeifer, C., & Wagner, J. (2012). Age and gender composition of the workforce, productivity and profits: Evidence from a new type of data for German enterprises. Productivity and Profits: Evidence from a New Type of Data for German Enterprises.

Pfeifer, C., & Wagner, J. (2014). Age and gender effects of workforce composition on productivity and profits: Evidence from a new type of data for German enterprises. Contemporary Economics, 8(1), 25–46.

Pontes, J., Geraldes, C. A., Fernandes, F. P., Sakurada, L., Rasmussen, A. L., Christiansen, L., Hafner-Zimmermann, S., Delaney, K., & Leitao, P. (2021). Relationship between Trends, Job Profiles, Skills, and Training Programs in the Factory of the Future. 2021 22nd IEEE International Conference on Industrial Technology (ICIT), 1, 1240–1245.

Ponton, M. K., & Rhea, N. E. (2006). Autonomous learning from a social cognitive perspective. New Horizons in Adult Education and Human Resource Development, 20(2), 38–49.

Poquet, O., & de Laat, M. (2021). Developing capabilities: Lifelong learning in the age of AI. British Journal of Educational Technology, 52(4), 1695–1708.

Pradhan, G. M. (2020). Job Design, Compensation and Commitment of Employee in Service Sector Organizations of Nepal. Management Dynamics, 23(2), 255–263.

Price, H. G. (1976). Achieving a balance between self-directed and required learning. Journal of Education for Social Work, 12(1), 105–112. 10.1080/00220612.1976.10671373.

Raemdonck, I., Gijbels, D., & Van Groen, W. (2014). The influence of job characteristics and self-directed learning orientation on workplace learning. International Journal of Training and Development, 18(3), 188–203.

Rajnai, Z., & Kocsis, I. (2017). Labor market risks of industry 4.0, digitization, robots, and AI. 2017 IEEE 15th International Symposium on Intelligent Systems and Informatics (SISY), 000343–000346.

Rangraz, M., & Pareto, L. (2021). Workplace work-integrated learning: supporting industry 4.0 transformation for small manufacturing plants by reskilling staff. International Journal of Lifelong Education, 40(1), 5–22. 10.1080/02601370.2020.1867249

Rashid, T., & Asghar, H. M. (2016). Technology use, self-directed learning, student engagement and academic performance: Examining the interrelations. Computers in Human Behavior, 63, 604–612. 10.1016/j.chb.2016.05.084

Rassameethes, B., Phusavat, K., Pastuszak, Z., Hidayanto, A. N., & Majava, J. (2021). From training to learning: Transition of a Workplace for Industry 4.0. Human Systems Management, (Preprint), 1–11. 10.3233/HSM-211533

Ratnawati, E., Sukidjo, S., & Efendi, R. (2020). The Effect of Work Motivation and Work Experience on Employee Performance. International Journal of Multicultural and Multireligious Understanding, 7(8), 109–116.

Reeves-Ellington, R., Palmer, G., & Nikolov, R. (2002). EMERGING COMMERCIALIZATION OF ELEARNING.

Regan, J. A. (2003). Motivating students towards self-directed learning. Nurse Education Today, 23(8), 593–599.

Rego, A., Sousa, F., Marques, C., & e Cunha, M. P. (2012). Authentic leadership promoting employees' psychological capital and creativity. Journal of Business Research, 65(3), 429–437.

Reinhart, C., & Reinhart, V. (2020). The pandemic depression: The global economy will never be the same. Foreign Aff., 99, 84.

Reio Jr, T. G., & Wiswell, A. (2000). Field investigation of the relationship among adult curiosity, workplace learning, and job performance. Human resource development quarterly, 11(1), 5–30. 10.1002/1532–1096(200021)11: 1<5:: AID-HRDQ2>3.0. CO;2-A

Richards, J. C. (2015). The changing face of language learning: Learning beyond the classroom. Relc Journal, 46(1), 5–22. 10.1177/0033688214561621

Richter, E., Brunner, M., & Richter, D. (2021). Teacher educators' task perception and its relationship to professional identity and teaching practice. Teaching and Teacher Education, 101, 103303.

Rigolizzo, M. (2019). Ready and willing to learn: Exploring personal antecedents to taking on learning challenges. Journal of Workplace Learning.

Robertson, C. (1995). NVQs: The impact of competence approaches. Management Development Review.

Robinson, G. (2021). Capturing a moving target: Interviewing fintech experts via LinkedIn. Area, 53(4), 671–678.

Rosmi, R., & Syamsir, S. (2020). The Influence of Integrity and Work Experience on Employee Performance. International Journal of Research and Analytical Reviews (IJRAR), 7(1), 789–794.

Ross, D. A. (2007). Backstage with the knowledge boys and girls: Goffman and distributed agency in an organic online community. Organization Studies, 28(3), 307–325.

Rowden, R. W. (2002). The relationship between workplace learning and job satisfaction in US small to midsize businesses. Human resource development quarterly, 13(4), 407–425. 10.1002/hrdq.1041

Ruczynski, L. I., van de Pol, M. H., Schouwenberg, B. J., Laan, R. F., & Fluit, C. R. (2022). Learning clinical reasoning in the workplace: a student perspective. BMC medical education, 22(1), 1–8. 10.1186/s12909–021–03083-y

Rusch, F. R., Hughes, C., Agran, M., Martin, J. E., & Johnson, J. R. (2009). Toward self-directed learning, post-high school placement, and coordinated support constructing new transition bridges to adult life. Career Development for Exceptional Individuals, 32(1), 53–59. 10.1177/0885728809332628

Ryder, M., Gallagher, P., Coughlan, B., Halligan, P., Guerin, S., & Connolly, M. (2022). Nursing and midwifery workforce readiness during a global pandemic: A survey of the experience of one hospital group in the Republic of Ireland. Journal of nursing management, 30(1), 25–32. 10.1111/jonm.13461

Saeid, N., & Eslaminejad, T. (2017). Relationship between Student's Self-Directed-Learning Readiness and Academic Self-Efficacy and Achievement Motivation in Students. International Education Studies, 10(1), 225–232.

Salili, F., Chiu, C., & Hong, Y. (2012). Student motivation: The culture and context of learning. Springer Science & Business Media.

Sandholtz, J. H. (2002). Inservice training or professional development: Contrasting opportunities in a school/university partnership. Teaching and teacher education, 18(7), 815–830. 10.1016/S0742–051X(02)00045–8

Santhanam, R., Sasidharan, S., & Webster, J. (2008). Using self-regulatory learning to enhance e-learning-based information technology training. Information Systems Research, 19(1), 26–47. 10.1287/isre.1070.0141

Sargeant, J., Armson, H., Chesluk, B., Dornan, T., Eva, K., Holmboe, E., ... & van der Vleuten, C. (2010). The processes and dimensions of informed self-assessment: a conceptual model. Academic Medicine, 85(7), 1212–1220. 10.1097/ACM.0b013e3181d85a4e

Sarmento, M. (2010). E-Learning as a tool to improve quality and productivity in hotels. Worldwide Hospitality and Tourism Themes.

Saunders, M., Lewis R. & Thronhill, A. (2009). Research Methods for business students. Fifth edition: Prentice Hall

Schermelleh-Engel, K., Moosbrugger, H., & Müller, H. (2003). Evaluating the fit of structural equation models: Tests of significance and descriptive goodness-of-fit measures. Methods of psychological research online, 8(2).

Schlegel, D., & Kraus, P. (2021). Skills and competencies for digital transformation–a critical analysis in the context of robotic process automation. International Journal of Organizational Analysis. 10.1108/IJOA-04–2021–2707

Schmidt, H. G., Vermeulen, L., & Van der Molen, H. T. (2006). Longterm effects of problem-based learning: a comparison of competencies acquired by graduates of a problem-based and a conventional medical school. Medical education, 40(6), 562–567. 10.1111/j.1365–2929.2006.02483.x

Schmidt, H., Van der Arend, A., Moust, J., Kokx, I., & Boon, L. (1993). Influence of tutors' subject-matter expertise on student effort and achievement in problem-based learning. Academic medicine, 68(10), 784–791. 10.1097/00001888–199310000–00018

Schönborn, G., Berlin, C., Pinzone, M., Hanisch, C., Georgoulias, K., & Lanz, M. (2019). Why social sustainability counts: The impact of corporate social sustainability culture on financial success. Sustainable Production and Consumption, 17, 1–10.

Schöttner, A. (2008). Relational contracts, multitasking, and job design. The Journal of Law, Economics, & Organization, 24(1), 138–162.

Schwienhorst, K. (2002). Why virtual, why environments? Implementing virtual reality concepts in computer-assisted language learning. Simulation & gaming, 33(2), 196–209.

Secundo, G., Gioconda, M., Del Vecchio, P., Gianluca, E., Margherita, A., & Valentina, N. (2021). Threat or opportunity? A case study of digital-enabled redesign of entrepreneurship education in the COVID-19 emergency. Technological forecasting and social change, 166, 120565. 10.1016/j.techfore.2020.120565

Serhan, S. A., & Yahaya, N. (2022). A Systematic Review and Trend Analysis of Personal Learning Environments Research. contexts, 7, 8. 10.18178/ijiet.2022.12.1.1585

Shamsi, S. Z., & Shobeiri, S. M. (2019). Mobile learning in environmental impact assessment training using theory of reasoned action. Research in Curriculum Planning, 16(60), 133–144.

Shantz, A., Alfes, K., Truss, C., & Soane, E. (2013). The role of employee engagement in the relationship between job design and task performance, citizenship and deviant behaviours. The International Journal of Human Resource Management, 24(13), 2608–2627.

Sheldon, K. M., & Elliot, A. J. (2000). Personal goals in social roles: Divergences and convergences across roles and levels of analysis. Journal of Personality, 68(1), 51–84.

Sheridan, I., Goggin, D., & Fallon, D. (2014). Facilitating External Engagement and Developing Industry-Focused Programmes in Cork Institute of Technology.

Shinagawa, N., Inada, T., Gomi, H., Akatsu, H., Yoshida, M., & Kawakami, Y. (2022). Challenges and experiences to develop a Japanese language course for international medical students in Japan: Maximising acquisition of Japanese language by applying adult learning theories.

Shintaku, K. (2022). Self-directed learning with anime: A case of Japanese language and culture. Foreign Language Annals. 10.1111/flan.12598

Shirom, A., Shechter Gilboa, S., Fried, Y., & Cooper, C. L. (2008). Gender, age and tenure as moderators of work-related stressors' relationships with job performance: A meta-analysis. Human Relations, 61(10), 1371–1398.

Shuval, J. T. (2000). The reconstruction of professional identity among immigrant physicians in three societies. Journal of Immigrant Health, 2(4), 191–202.

Sim, M.-J., & Oh, H.-S. (2012). Influence of self efficacy, learning motivation, and self-directed learning on problem-solving ability in nursing students. The Journal of the Korea Contents Association, 12(6), 328–337.

Simões, A. C., Ferreira, F., Almeida, A., Zimmermann, R., Castro, H., & Azevedo, A. (2021, November). Innovative Learning Scheme to Up-skilling and Re-skilling–Designing a Collaborative Training Program between Industry and Academia towards Digital Transformation. In Working Conference on Virtual Enterprises (pp. 729–737). Springer, Cham. 10.1007/978-3-030-85969-5-69

Simonton, D. K. (2014). Creative performance, expertise acquisition, individual differences, and developmental antecedents: An integrative research agenda. Intelligence, 45, 66–73.

Singh, S., & Ehlers, S. (2021). Employability as a global norm: Comparing transnational employability policies of OECD, ILO, World Bank Group, and UNESCO. International and Comparative Studies in Adult and Continuing Education, 131.

Skager, R. (1979). Self-directed learning and schooling: Identifying pertinent theories and illustrative research. International Review of Education, 25(4), 517–543. 10.1007/BF00598508

Slotnick, H. B. (1999). How doctors learn: physicians' self-directed learning episodes. Acad Med, 74(10), 1106–1117. 10.1097/00001888–199910000–00014

Smith, J. K., & Heshusius, L. (1986). Closing down the conversation: The end of the quantitative-qualitative debate among educational inquirers. Educational researcher, 15(1), 4–12.

Soldatos, J., Kefalakis, N., Makantasis, G., Marguglio, A., & Lazaro, O. (2021, September). Digital Platform and Operator 4.0 Services for Manufacturing Repurposing During COVID19. In IFIP International Conference on Advances in Production Management Systems (pp. 311–320). Springer, Cham. 10.1007/978-3-030-85910-7-33

Song, L., & Hill, J. R. (2007). A conceptual model for understanding self-directed learning in online environments. Journal of Interactive Online Learning, 6(1), 27–42.

Song, Y., Lee, Y., & Lee, J. (2022). Mediating effects of self-directed learning on the relationship between critical thinking and problem-solving in student nurses attending online classes: A cross-sectional descriptive study. Nurse education today, 109, 105227. 10.1016/j.nedt.2021.105227

Soule, D. L., Puram, A., Westerman, G. F., & Bonnet, D. (2016). Becoming a digital organization: The journey to digital dexterity. Available at SSRN 2697688.

Srinivasan, M., Wilkes, M., Stevenson, F., Nguyen, T., & Slavin, S. (2007). Comparing problem-based learning with case-based learning: effects of a major curricular shift at two institutions. Academic Medicine, 82(1), 74–82. 10.1097/01.ACM.0000249963.93776.aa

Steiger, J. H. (2007), "Understanding the limitations of global fit assessment in structural equation modeling," Personality and Individual Differences, 42 (5).

Stephany, F. (2020). Does it Pay Off to Learn a New Skill? Revealing the Economic Benefits of Cross-Skilling. SSRN Electronic Journal.

Stephany, F. (2021). One size does not fit all: Constructing complementary digital reskilling strategies using online labour market data. Big Data & Society, 8(1), 20539517211003120.

Strack, R., Carrasco, M., Kolo, P., Nouri, N., Priddis, M., & George, R. (2021). The Future of Jobs in the Era of AI.

Stringer, J. K., Gruppen, L. D., Ryan, M. S., Ginzburg, S. B., Cutrer, W. B., Wolff, M., & Santen, S. A. (2022). Measuring the Master Adaptive Learner: Development and Internal Structure Validity Evidence for a New Instrument. Medical Science Educator, 1–11.

Sung, E. (2017). The Relationship Between Life-Learning Competency and Self-Directed Learning Ability, Problem-Solving Ability, and Academic Achievement of University Students in the Context of Higher Education. Educational Technology International, 18(2), 249–263.

Swisher, V. (2013). Learning agility: The "X" factor in identifying and developing future leaders. Industrial and Commercial Training.

Tabachnick, B. G., & Fidell, L. S. (2007). Using Multivariate statistics (5th edition), Boston: Pearson/Allyn & Bacon

Tao, Y., Li, L., Xu, Q., & Jiang, A. (2015). Development of a nursing education program for improving Chinese undergraduates' self-directed learning: A mixed-method study. Nurse Education Today, 35(11), 1119–1124.

Tarus, B. K. (2014). Effects of Job Rotation Strategy on High Performance Workplace, in Lake Victoria North Water Services Board, Kenya. International Journal of Business and Management, 9(11), 139.

Taylor, D., & Miflin, B. (2008). Problem-based learning: where are we now?. Medical teacher, 30(8), 742–763. 10.1080/01421590802217199

Templeton, G. F., Lewis, B. R., & Snyder, C. A. (2002). Development of a measure for the organizational learning construct. Journal of Management Information Systems, 19(2), 175–218.

ten Cate, O. T. J., Kusurkar, R. A., & Williams, G. C. (2011). How self-determination theory can assist our understanding of the teaching and learning processes in medical education. AMEE guide No. 59. Medical teacher, 33(12), 961–973. 10.3109/0142159X.2011.595435

Teo, A. S. C. (Ed.). (2021). Univer-cities: Reshaping Strategies To Meet Radical Change, Pandemics And Inequality-Revisiting The Social Compact?-Volume Iv. World Scientific. 10.1142/12207

Teo, T. S., Lim, V. K., & Lai, R. Y. (1999). Intrinsic and extrinsic motivation in Internet usage. Omega, 27(1)

Thompson, D. J. (2013). Understanding the contextual, cultural, and individual antecedents of self-directed development. The University of Akron.

Thongmak, M. (2021). A model for enhancing employees' lifelong learning intention online. Learning and Motivation, 75, 101733.

Thorndike, E. L., Bregman, E. O., Tilton, J., & Woodyard, E. (1928). Adult learning.

Tillema, H. H. (2000). Belief change towards self-directed learning in student teachers: immersion in practice or reflection on action. Teaching and teacher education, 16(5–6), 575–591. 10.1016/S0742–051X(00)00016–0

Toiviainen, H., Sadik, S., Bound, H., Pasqualoni, P. P., & Ramsamy-Prat, P. (2021). Dimensions of expansion for configuring learning spaces in global work. Journal of Workplace Learning. 10.1108/JWL-11–2020–0182

Trede, F., Macklin, R., & Bridges, D. (2012). Professional identity development: a review of the higher education literature. Studies in higher education, 37(3), 365-384. 10.1080/03075079.2010.521237

Trout, G. (2016). E-learning & online training. Professional Safety, 61(6), 34.

Tsou, M.-W., & Yang, C.-H. (2019). Does gender structure affect firm productivity? Evidence from China. China Economic Review, 55, 19–36.

Tull, D. S. & Hawkins, D. I. (1993). Marketing research: measurement & method. New York: Macmillan Publishing.

Valenti, C. (2021). The protection of professionalism in the changing labor market. Labor and Law, 35 (1), 131–154. 10.1441/100283

Vallerand, R. J. (1997). Toward a hierarchical model of intrinsic and extrinsic motivation. Advances in experimental social psychology, 29.

Van de Wiel, M. W., Van den Bossche, P., Janssen, S., & Jossberger, H. (2011). Exploring deliberate practice in medicine: how do physicians learn in the workplace?. Advances in health sciences education, 16(1), 81–95. 10.1007/s10459–010–9246–3

Van Gelderen, M. (2010). Autonomy as the guiding aim of entrepreneurship education. Education+ Training. 10.1108/00400911011089006

Venables, A. J. (2016). Using natural resources for development: Why has it proven so difficult? Journal of Economic Perspectives, 30(1), 161–184.

Venkatesh, V., Speier, C. (1999). Computer technology training in the workplace: A longitudinal investigation of the effect of mood. Organizational Behavior and Human Decision Processes, 79(1).

Verma, A., & Venkatesan, M. (2021). Industry 4.0 workforce implications and strategies for organisational effectiveness in Indian automotive industry: a review. Technology Analysis & Strategic Management, 1–9. 10.1080/09537325.2021.2007875

Vijayashree, P., & Chandran, M. (2018). Empirical Evidences for Effectiveness of Employee Participation in IT Companies. Indian Journal of Public Health Research & Development, 9(10).

Vinokur, A. D., Price, R. H., & Caplan, R. D. (1996). Hard times and hurtful partners: How financial strain affects depression and relationship satisfaction of unemployed persons and their spouses. Journal of Personality and Social Psychology, 71(1), 166.

Wagner, E. (2006). Delivering on the Promise of eLearning. Adobe. Com.

Wainer, A. L., & Ingersoll, B. R. (2015). Increasing access to an ASD imitation intervention via a telehealth parent training program. Journal of autism and developmental disorders, 45(12), 3877–3890. 10.1007/s10803–014–2186–7

Wallo, A., Kock, H., Reineholm, C., & Ellström, P. E. (2021). How do managers promote workplace learning? Learning-oriented leadership in daily work. Journal of Workplace Learning. 10.1108/JWL-11–2020–0176

Wang, H. C., & Chen, C. W. Y. (2020). Learning English from YouTubers: English L2 learners' self-regulated language learning on YouTube. Innovation in Language Learning and Teaching, 14(4), 333–346. 10.1080/17501229.2019.1607356

Wang, S., & Zhang, X. (2022). Impact mechanism of supervisor developmental feedback on employee workplace learning. Managerial and Decision Economics, 43(1), 219–227. 10.1002/mde.3379

Waqanimaravu, M., & Arasanmi, C. N. (2020). Employee training and service quality in the hospitality industry. Journal of Foodservice Business Research, 23(3), 216–227.

Wasityastuti, W., Susani, Y. P., Prabandari, Y. S., & Rahayu, G. R. (2018). Correlation between academic motivation and professional identity in medical students in the Faculty of Medicine of the Universitas Gadjah Mada Indonesia. Educación Médica, 19(1), 23–29.

Watson, G. J., Desouza, K. C., Ribiere, V. M., & Lindič, J. (2021). Will AI ever sit at the C-suite Table? The future of senior leadership. Business Horizons, 64(4), 465–474. 10.1016/j.bushor.2021.02.011

Webb, J. (2021). Learning in lockdown: A case study in rapid transition to remote teaching. Business Information Review, 38(1), 15–20. 10.1177/0266382120984731

Webb, R. (1985). A case of information skills: re-skilling or de-skilling?. Cambridge Journal of Education, 15(2), 81–87. 10.1080/0305764850150203

Webster-Wright, A. (2009). Reframing professional development through understanding authentic professional learning. Review of educational research, 79(2), 702–739. 10.3102/0034654308330970

White, S. (2004). What motivates them? Some adult learners' perceptions of and reasons for engaging in lifelong learning.

Whittington, R., Molloy, E., Mayer, M., & Smith, A. (2006). Practices of strategising/organising: Broadening strategy work and skills. Long Range Planning, 39(6), 615–629.

Wilson, F. M. (2018). Organizational behaviour and work: A critical introduction. Oxford university press.

Wilson, K. M., & Halpin, E. (2006). Convergence and professional identity in the academic library. Journal of Librarianship and Information Science, 38(2), 79–91.

Wilson, N., & Syed, H. H. (2021). Employees Relevancy Following The Emergence of Artificial Intelligence (AI). Artificial Intelligence (AI), 11(9), 1692–1701.

Wisecarver, M., Foldes, H., Ferro, G., Cullen, M., Graves, T. R., Rauchfuss, G., Wolfson, N., & Kraiger, K. (2012). Defining antecedents for noncommissioned officer self-learning: A review of the literature.

Wisman, J. D. (2010). The moral imperative and social rationality of government-guaranteed employment and reskilling. Review of Social Economy, 68(1), 35–67.

Woltering, V., Herrler, A., Spitzer, K., & Spreckelsen, C. (2009). Blended learning positively affects students' satisfaction and the role of the tutor in the problem-based learning process: results of a mixed-method evaluation. Advances in Health Sciences Education, 14(5), 725–738. 10.1007/s10459–009–9154–6

Wright, T. A., & Bonett, D. G. (2002). The moderating effects of employee tenure on the relation between organizational commitment and job performance: A meta-analysis. Journal of Applied Psychology, 87(6), 1183.

Wu, Z. (2020). China's Experiences in Developing Lifelong Education, 1978–2017. ECNU Review of Education, 2096531120953959.

Xiaoquan, P. A. N., & Huijuan, S. (n.d.). Understanding factors influencing EFL students' technology-based self-directed learning. International Journal of Social Sciences and Education Research, 6(4), 450–459.

Yang, S. C., & Chen, Y. J. (2007). Technology-enhanced language learning: A case study. Computers in human behavior, 23(1), 860–879. 10.1016/j.chb.2006.02.015

Yap, J. S., & Tan, J. (2022). Lifelong learning competencies among chemical engineering students at Monash University Malaysia during the COVID-19 pandemic. Education for Chemical Engineers, 38, 60–69.

Yilmaz, R. (2017). Exploring the role of e-learning readiness on student satisfaction and motivation in flipped classroom. Computers in Human Behavior, 70, 251–260. 10.1016/j.chb.2016.12.085

Yim, K.-H., & Lee, I. (2021). The effect of achievement motivation on learning agility of nursing students: The mediating effect of self-leadership. The Journal of Korean Academic Society of Nursing Education, 27(1), 80–90.

Young, J. Q., Van Merrienboer, J., Durning, S., & Ten Cate, O. (2014). Cognitive load theory: implications for medical education: AMEE Guide No. 86. Medical teacher, 36(5), 371–384. 10.3109/0142159X.2014.889290

Yuhui, H., & Hongxin, L. (2014). Self-directed learning and the effectiveness of e-learning in enterprises. International Journal of E-Education, e-Business, e-Management and e-Learning, 4(3), 187.

Zahidi, S. (2020). We need a global reskilling revolution–here's why. World Economic Forum, 22.

Zakaria, A. F., Mohamed, M., & Mohamad, M. M. (2021). Efforts to Improve Knowledge and Skills by Adopting Heutagogical Approaches among Technical and Vocational'Educators. Journal of Technical Education and Training, 13(3), 172–179. 10.30880/jtet.2021.13.03.017

Zareie, B., & Navimipour, N. J. (2016). The effect of electronic learning systems on the employee's commitment. The International Journal of Management Education, 14(2), 167–175.

Zhang, X., Liao, H., Li, N., & Colbert, A. E. (2020). Playing it safe for my family: Exploring the dual effects of family motivation on employee productivity and creativity. Academy of Management Journal, 63(6), 1923–1950.

Zhang, Y., & Perkins, D. D. (2022). Toward an Empowerment Model of Community Education in China. Adult Education Quarterly, 07417136211062252.

Zhu, M., Bonk, C. J., & Doo, M. Y. (2020). Self-directed learning in MOOCs: Exploring the relationships among motivation, self-monitoring, and self-management. Educational Technology Research and Development, 68(5), 2073–2093. 10.1007/s11423-020-09747-8

Zide, J., Elman, B., & Shahani-Denning, C. (2014). LinkedIn and recruitment: How profiles differ across occupations. Employee Relations.

Zikmund, W. G. (2000). Business research methods (6th ed.). Fort Worth, TX: Thomson/South-W

Zimmerman, B. J., & Lebeau, R. B. (2000). A commentary on self-directed learning. Problem-Based Learning: A Research Perspective on Learning Interactions, 299–313.

List of Abbreviations

4IR	Fourth Industrial Revolution
ADMIN	Administration
AGFI	Adjusted Goodness of Fit Index
AI	Artificial Intelligence
AI/ML	Artificial Intelligence and Machine Learning
AMOS	Analysis Of Moment Structures
AR	Augmented Reality
ARCS	Attention, Relevance, Confidence and Satisfaction
AVE	Average Variance Extracted
BI	Behavioural Intention
BPBL	Blended Problem Based Learning
CAGR	Compound Annual Growth Rate
CBL	Case Based Learning
CFA	Confirmatory Factor Analysis
CFI	Comparative Fit Index
CMM	Capability Maturity Model
CXO	Chief Experience Officer
DF	Degree Of Freedom
DIY	Do-It-Yourself
DTPB	Decomposed Theory of Planned Behaviour
EI	Emotional Intelligence

ELEARNING	Electronic Learning
G20	Global 20
GDP	Gross Domestic Product
GFI	Goodness Of Fit Index
GUI	Graphical User Interface
HR	Human Resources
ICT	Information And Communication Technology
IDEA	Industrial Development and Educational Assessment
ILO	International Labour Organization
SEM	Structural Equation Modelling
SIG	Significant
SPSS	Statistical Package of Social Sciences
SRL	Self-Regulated Learning
SSM	Self-Skilling Model
STEM	Science, Technology, Engineering, And Management
TAM	Technology Adoption Model
TLI	Tucker Lewis Index
TPB	Theory Of Planned Behaviour
TRA	Theory Of Reasoned Action
TWA	Theory Of Work Adjustment
UN	United Nations
UNESCO	United National Educational, Scientific, And Cultural Organization
USD	United States Dollar
VUCA	Volatile Uncertain Complex and Ambiguous
WEF	World Economic Forum
WPL	Workplace Learning

About the Author

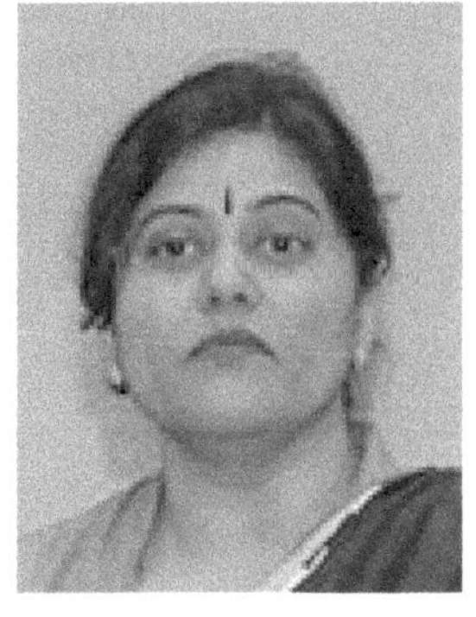

Dr. Deepa V Mukherjee is a human resource leadership pioneer and an inspiration in talent management. With roots in organizational development and a flair for applied neuroscience, Dr. Deepa's approach to people development is both heartfelt and groundbreaking.

With over 15 years in pivotal leadership roles and almost three decades in the industry, she is currently spearheading the people agenda for a leading high-tech product firm in India. She is a changemaker who has been listed among the country's Top CHROs, Talent Development Leaders and celebrated as a shining HR Tech Mind.

Dr. Deepa's foresight led her to explore social sustainability, lifelong learning, and the dynamics of employment, earning her a PhD in Management. Her work isn't confined to academia – it is lived and breathed in companies and showcased in her inventive Career Sustainability Assessment (CSA)® Tool and the transformative Employee Self-Skilling (ESSM)® model.

Awards like the Indian Achievers' Award and the "Iconic Women Creating a Better World for All" honour from the Women Economic Forum in 2022 are testaments to her impact. Dr. Deepa's most heartfelt project is ME Green India. Born from her PhD research, it is a call to action for career self-governance and a sustainable work world for everyone- a world where professional growth meets sustainability.